Parenting Your
TEEN
and Loving It

Parenting Your
TEEN
and Loving It

Being the Mom Your Kid Needs

SUSIE DAVIS

Revell

a division of Baker Publishing Group
Grand Rapids, Michigan

© 2009 by Susie Davis

Published by Revell
a division of Baker Publishing Group
P.O. Box 6287, Grand Rapids, MI 49516-6287
www.revellbooks.com

Printed in the United States of America

Library of Congress Cataloging-in-Publication Data
Davis, Susie, 1963–
    Parenting your teen and loving it : being the mom your kid needs / Susie Davis.
      p. cm.
    Includes bibliographical references.
    ISBN 978-0-8007-3318-6 (pbk.)
    1. Mother and child—Religious aspects—Christianity. 2. Parent and teenager—Religious aspects—Christianity. 3. Parenting—Religious aspects—Christianity. I. Title.
BV4529.18.D38 2009
248.8′431—dc22
                                            2008054965

To protect the privacy of those whose stories are shared in this book, some details and names have been changed.

For Will 3, Emily, and Sara

And now I entrust you to God and the message of his grace that is able to build you up and give you an inheritance with all those he has set apart for himself.

Acts 20:32

Contents

Acknowledgments

How could I begin to write a book on parenting teenagers without some serious help from my team of resident experts?

A huge and heartfelt thanks to you, Will 3, for being my firstborn and my unwitting guinea pig. Thank you for your grace as I stumbled through parenting as best I could. Thank you for putting up with all my trial and error, for saying nary a word when I raised my voice unnecessarily, and for turning out just fabulously despite it all. I couldn't be prouder of the man you've become, and I honestly look forward to you completing your degree in psychology so you can analyze all my quirks. I love you.

Emily, sweet girl, you completely broke the mold on goodness. Thank you for being the most conscientious, considerate, non-emotional teenager alive. I can't imagine this house without your loud, carefree singing or your weird, wacky dance moves. From the bottom of my heart—thanks for the joy! I love you.

Sara—as you well know, I think you are the coolest superfreak ever. Thank you for being just perfectly Sara, our little Indian girl. I promise, to the best of my ability, not to overprotect, overmanage, or overmother you your last four years at home. So peace out, baby girl. I love you.

And of course, I must thank Will, my husband of twenty-three years. Without whom I would not have this blessed job parenting teens in the first place. Thank you for seeing me through yet another writing season. Thank you for loving Jesus. I love you.

I must also include the people behind the scenes who have helped stage this ministry writing production. Thanks to Diahn Ehlers, without whom I would be sitting and staring at a blank screen. Thank you for encouraging me, analyzing my thoughts, and giving me a leg up when I was thrown to the ground. I am immensely grateful for your gift of training the writer in me. For Jodi Allen, who not only read every chapter but responded with heartfelt vulnerability, you constantly reminded me why I was writing the book in the first place. Thanks to Jillynn Shaver, my prayer partner and reader. Thank you for your words of encouragement for my writing but more importantly for comforting my soul in the dark night. Though I still miss the audible, I know the anointing. To Liz Benigno—my original Zuzu friend, thank you for praying and reading and always being there when I need you. I count your friendship as a blessing. And finally, thank you to Holly Floyd for jumping in and agreeing to read my manuscript. Your vast experience with the students at Hyde Park and as a mother of grown children greatly enriched my writing.

And where would I be without Bill Jensen? My amazing agent—a man with patience, insight, and quite the sense of humor. Thank you for managing my energy and my ideas with such wisdom.

Lastly, I am greatly indebted to the team at Revell. Thank you for partnering in ministry to encourage moms everywhere.

Introduction

Parenting Your Teen and Loving It

Teenagers. You gotta love them. Bursting with energy, wild with idealism, and filled to overflowing with hormones. And yet there is nothing like a teenager to baffle and bewilder a mother. It seems that just about the time you get some effective parenting techniques down, that sweet-faced ten-year-old turns into a gangly teenager, creating a whole new set of issues. Their questions are endless, matching the frequency (but not the delight) of a curious, insistent two-year-old. They want to know why they have to do homework, why they have to do chores, and why you are wearing such nerdy clothes. It's a confusing time for a mother. In the flash of an eye, the little darlings seemingly morph into little devils, causing the most saintly of mothers to confess, "My teenager is driving me crazy!"

The extreme moodiness, indifferent attitudes, and bizarre behaviors of a teenager can create what feels like shipwreck for the parent/child relationship. The emotional upset can practically hurl a mother overboard as the stormy seas of adolescence replace the calm, controlled waters of childhood. This shift in season creates challenges a mother never imagined. Whether it's teenage rebellion or just hormonal absentmindedness, the seas are stirred, and a mother suddenly realizes she must learn a new skill set to safely reach the other side.

A mother knows that in order to effectively influence, she must not antagonize her teenager. She grasps the reality that the last years at home are extremely crucial. And most importantly, she understands that a positive and loving presence is essential to helping her adolescent avert the dangerous waters of teen culture. So she presses past the exhaustion, the thanklessness, and the confusion, knowing these are critical years in a very chaotic time for her child.

It is up to her to be the most loving, patient, and wise mother she can be, no matter what the cost. And she knows she must not bail out, no matter how confusing the relationship becomes.

Parenting Your Teen and Loving It honestly faces the challenges of mothering the modern teenager. It addresses the need to proactively parent while attempting to have a positive relationship at the same time. The book provides explanations about the physical and emotional development of teenagers while giving biblical guidelines for healthy interaction and leadership. But most important, the book seeks to improve the way a mother actually feels toward her teenagers—enabling her to love and appreciate them with real affection—which will give her the relationship she truly desires.

Section One

A Purposeful
MOM

~ full of determination ~

Missing in Action

That Teen Is No Longer Your Baby

My teenager, Emily, is at her friend Margo's house tonight. I have called her cell several times to check in on them because I am a little concerned. Emily told me about her plan for the evening, but it seems to keep changing. And the longer she is gone, the more my imagination is running away with me. You see, Emily and Margo decided to dye their hair . . . blue. Well, Emily is going for blue. Margo decided on pink because it matches her skin tone better.

This all came up late last week, and I have to say it was a conversation I never expected to have with Emily.

"Mom, is it OK with you if I go over to Margo's next weekend?" she asked innocently enough.

"Well, sure, Emily. That's great," I answered, smiling.

Long ago I decided Margo is the perfect friend for Emily. She's a serious student, has great morals, is cheerful, polite, and comes from a fabulous family. Why wouldn't I want Emily to spend time at Margo's next weekend? I could think of no reason whatsoever. That is until Emily blurted out the next few words.

"OK—great! See, Margo and I decided we are going to dye our hair this weekend. We're going to streak it blue and pink. You're OK with that, right, Mom? It's not like it will stay that way forever, because, you know, it will grow out someday. We're going to have so much fun. You know?"

"Um . . . what?!" I was startled by her suggestion. This is the very same Emily that denied an offer by her mother some months previous for professional highlights. Er, blonde highlights, that is. Why, she was actually offended that I had

All my babies are gone now. I say this not in sorrow but in disbelief. I take great satisfaction in what I have today: three almost-adults, two taller than I am, one closing in fast. Three people who read the same books I do and have learned not to be afraid of disagreeing with me in their opinion of them, who sometimes tell vulgar jokes that make me laugh until I choke and cry, who need razor blades and shower gel and privacy, who want to keep their doors closed more than I like. Who, miraculously, go to the bathroom, zip up their jackets, and move food from plate to mouth all by themselves. Like the trick soap I bought for the bathroom with a rubber ducky at its center, the baby is buried deep within each, barely discernible except through the unreliable haze of the past.[1]

Anna Quindlen, *Loud and Clear*

asked. "No, Mom! I will never highlight my hair! Everyone does that and it looks so fake!" So to say it took me off guard when she told me about her plans with Margo is somewhat of an understatement. I had no idea she would be remotely interested in blue, pink, or what eventually became purple hair. None whatsoever.

When Mom Needs a Makeover

The thing I need to constantly remember is that Emily is no longer a little girl; she's a teenager. And though I might still have her permanently pictured in my mind at four years old—long curly locks with an impish, infectious grin—she is no longer that tiny thing. She is eighteen, a year from attending college, and quite the independent thinker. She's really a fabulous person. I genuinely admire who she is and who she's becoming—magenta streaks and all. But it takes a lot of perspective to continually view her as the nearly grown-up and not the little girl. It is very easy for me to allow myself to act and react like the mother I was to her when she was four and even fourteen, not who she is today at eighteen.

That's really the tricky part of parenting people, isn't it? Managing the constant growth. And I don't mean that it's difficult for me to manage Emily's constant physical growth. That happens without me doing anything at all. She grows at lightning speed, changing like the weather. What I mean is that it's hard for me to manage *my growth as a mother on her behalf.* I'm the one with growing pains, and frankly, I'm the one in need of a makeover. Because the truth is, as Emily transforms before my eyes, my mothering must transform also. I can no longer expect to use the same bag of tricks that I used when she was a toddler or a ten-year-old. I must continually seek help from God about how to effectively parent this person in front of me. The person she is today—not the person she was yesterday or even the person she will someday become, but the person standing in front of me today. It can seem an intense task.

As a matter of fact, when you consider all the change a teen is going through—physically, emotionally, intellectually, and spiritually—keeping pace with an appropriate parental curriculum can be downright stressful. And when you add to that the fact that parents themselves are grappling with demanding jobs, a spousal relationship, and aging parents, the added teen agenda can flood a parent with feelings of inadequacy altogether. It's not just that parents don't know how in the world to deal with this new teenage persona, they are finding it increasingly difficult to find the time and energy to deal with it all. The last thing a mother wants is to feel like she has to re-create her parenting style to manage the emerging teenager in her house, but . . . that is exactly what is needed.

Scientists have studied the behavior and emotions of parents as well as their adolescent children, and found that when children reach puberty, parents experience tremendous changes in themselves. What's more, they shift their attitudes toward their children. It isn't just the kids who are distressed. Parents are too.[2]

Virginia Rutter, "Whose Hell Is It? Why the Turbulent Teens Are So Tough on Families"

What's at Risk?

The problem with ignoring the necessity of a mom makeover is that there are things at risk—great risk. If a mom decides that she simply can't change or conform to what the preteen/teen really needs, she risks antagonizing and isolating the kid, creating a disconnect in the relationship. When we as mothers fail the parenting challenge that stares us in the face, we place the relationship we have nurtured for some ten-plus years in a dangerous place. It's dangerous because we desire a close relationship with our growing children and we threaten to disrupt it when we're inflexible. But it's also dangerous because teenagers desperately need appropriate mothering during the angst of adolescence.

When we don't grow in our parenting style, keeping pace with the speed and needs of the changing adolescent, we quickly become parenting dinosaurs. Outdated—unable to keep up. And though a teenager might slam the door in your face, leaving you wishing for a tame ten-year-old, she will be deeply grateful for a forward-thinking mom who helps her navigate the decisions ahead. She doesn't need to find a mother unfit for the challenge because of a staunch disbelief that her baby is growing up. Instead, she needs to find a mom who understands and celebrates the unique changes ahead. A mom who is exceptionally insightful where teens are concerned—and that would be you!

The Perfect Download

Wouldn't it be great if there was a universal parenting curriculum? Kind of a one size fits all. What if God gave a single parenting download package that fit every child at every stage of life no matter what? Oh, life would be sweet. My mothering confidence would soar. I would make decisions instantaneously, resolved that I always did everything just perfectly. And I could justify that when things were amiss, it was certainly no fault of mine! But that just hasn't been my experience—because there isn't a once-in-a-lifetime download. Instead, I find I need a constant download of new information. I regularly deal with parenting inadequacy in the monumental task of raising my teenagers. I often wonder about the decisions I make, and like any mother, I shoulder my share of the mother lode of good old-fashioned guilt. It seems that just about the time I think things are zooming along—with a healthy, happy teenager—a situation arises that sends me directly to my knees, in need of another parenting download appropriate to the situation.

But you know what . . . that's just where I should be. In a position of continually asking God for help in raising these precious teenagers he has given me. It's the desperation of needing God in my life that wakens my spiritual perspective. When I feel tired and confused and I wonder what kind of mother I really am, I get very needy before God. I am needy of his grace and guidance. And I am painfully aware that I need God's help constantly for me to be the person my teenagers need.

But do you know how God responds to a tired, confused, sometimes overwhelmed mother of teenagers? With grace. In 2 Corinthians 12:9, God promises, "My grace is all you need. My power works best in weakness." Isn't that amazing? Realizing that God takes my weakness and uses it as a vehicle for his power is an overwhelming relief.

If I want to get the perfect parenting download, I come to God just as I am. I lay down my frustrations and my fears, and I seek God's power through my weakness.

The truth is, God has equipped us for every season and role in life. He holds the keys to successfully parenting the teenager set before us. And it is with his help that we can have the confident assurance as mothers that we are moving in the right direction. It is with his help we can genuinely love our teenagers (magenta locks and all) with an irresistible, unconditional love. He will provide the direction for becoming all we need to be for the sake of the teen/mother relationship and for the sake of raising a productive, God-loving young person. We have access to what we as mothers need most: more, more, more of God and his wisdom and grace.

So if you need perspective for the ever-changing role of mothering a teenager, then jump right in. And begin the process of learning about how to become the mother you always dreamed of—without going crazy in the process.

■ ■ ■ ■ ■ ■ ■ ■

PARENTING YOUR TEEN

- What are the signs in your family that might indicate you are in need of a makeover? Were you aware that you would need to revamp your parenting style to manage your teen?
- How might declining a makeover create craziness in your family?

- Why does mothering a teenager seem to be one of the most demanding parenting tasks?
- How is a mother's job parenting a teenager much different than a father's job parenting a teenager?
- What do you do when you feel like a "weak" mother? How could you redirect your efforts and become a more confident mother?

A Proven Parenting Plan

The Relationship Strategy

George Barna, of the Barna Research Group, recently un-covered some startling statistics. He surveyed parents and found two commonalities: the first is the fact that most parents want to do a great job raising their kids, and the second is that the majority of those parents have no plan for accomplishing the goal.[1] Sounds pretty impractical, but apparently, parents everywhere are entering the enormous job of raising kids just hoping that somehow, in the mix from zero to eighteen, little junior will end up becoming a healthy young adult.

In his book *Revolutionary Parenting*, Barna points out that most parents resort to "de facto" strategies, which include among other things preparing a child for success by handing them over to the experts and protecting them from insecure environments that place them in harm's way.[2] And while these are worthy avenues for parents to prep their youngsters to adulthood, Barna notes that the most critical component in a child's world isn't a master teacher or a risk-free environment. The most significant—and overlooked—factor in a child's world is a rich relational bond with Mom and Dad. When you boil it all down to the bare basics, the best parenting plan possible is a good relationship. It's not the best school or most well-rounded extracurricular schedule. It's not living in the "right" neighborhood or having the widest social circle. It's not having all the toys or trips that bring life's most fulfilling experiences. It's just you and your child.

Now, if you are reading this and your kids are say, in the nine-to-ten-year-old range, you might be thinking, "Piece of cake! Check that off—is that all there is?!" Okay, understood. You feel that because your brood believes the sun rises and sets as a result of your very existence, your job here is done. Because, of course, your kids still delight in your presence when you stop by their school at lunchtime and invite you to squeeze in next to them to share a peanut butter sandwich. They are relieved when you're the carpool mom, because they hold secret notions that not only are they safest with you but you are the coolest mom too. And at night, they'll still cuddle close and let you read to them after they beg for just one more chapter of *Stuart Little*. They'll probably fall asleep listening to your soothing voice, believing all is well with the world. So yes,

> A goal without a plan is just a wish.
>
> Antoine de Saint-Exupery

you can confidently state that the relationship is a piece of cake, because you believe that your child is securely tethered forever. But enter the teen years when that child becomes, say, twelve or thirteen, maybe fourteen—in which case all bets are off. Because at that point, being a cool carpool mom is the least effective part of your relationship.

When a child becomes a teenager, the parent/child relationship shifts. In the younger years, the vitality of the relationship centers around the basic tenet that when Mom is lovingly providing for the child's needs, Mom is fulfilling the relationship needs. When a child is young, the relationship centers around you, the mom, *doing things* to help the child. Say, like tackling schoolwork or shuffling after-school schedules. And then there's all that dirty laundry they generate— you're doing loads of that. You're caring for their physical health by scheduling and maintaining well checks with the pediatrician and caring for the little ones when they get the croup at two o'clock in the morning. You cart them to and from play dates with friends and plan birthday parties. And they regard you with adoring adulation because you are the gatekeeper to their well-being. But when they become teenagers, that "child" might begin to look at you through a completely different lens.

Well, yes, you—the mother—drive them to and from school, but that's because it's *your job*. And sure, you clean all their clothes and take them to the doctor, but *don't all moms do that*? When this slow, insidious shift takes place, the worst thing you can do as a mother is to keep insisting that the relationship is all about your *role* as their mother, while neglecting to understand the *relationship*. Because the truth is that your relationship is a completely different animal altogether than your role in their life, and though the two remain intermixed in your mind, they come to stand alone for your teen.

New Levels of Mastery

Understanding this relational shift is *the* way to ensure that the relationship stands strong in the teen years. If you neglect to shift your awareness in this area, you will be left behind as your teen surges forward into independence. And yet this creates a very real tension for a mother, because as the rules change, you're not quite sure who is holding the handbook. While you notice the subtle changes in the relationship ("Mom, please don't come to the lunchroom if I forget my lunch. Leave it in the office, OK?"), you don't remember exactly when things changed so much. Sure, you get the whole teen development deal and you remember your own mother driving you crazy when you were fourteen, but somehow it absolutely blindsides you when it occurs with your own child. It's the eye rolling, the slouchy attitude, and the nonverbal disdain for all things motherly. Frankly, it's easy to get your feelings hurt. You don't know what the rules of the relationship look like, and if we're honest, neither does your child. You are both, in a sense, needing new levels and insights of mastering the parent/child relationship.

I know there were many times I bungled it with my firstborn, Will 3, now twenty-one. When he was thirteen, I kept trying to *do* things the same way—enriching the relationship by caring for him. Waking him up, fixing him breakfast, asking him about his day . . . and it was met with increasing irritation. He didn't want a kiss on the forehead in the morning any more than he wanted a plate of hot scrambled eggs and toast. And he certainly didn't want to *talk* first thing in the morning about the details of his day. The quieter he got, the more I pressed in, varying breakfast choices and trying to be less chatty but still just as prominent. I was struggling to understand my place with Will. I felt like the relationship was slipping away every time he pushed away from the plate, both figuratively and literally. I sensed in my gut that I should back off, but I didn't know where to go. Because I knew that he needed me—as any teenager truly does need an attentive mother; however, I just couldn't find a place that was comfortable for both of us. I was ready to serve but unable to connect. I desperately needed to transition my skills as a mother. And what I now know is that I needed to move my relationship from *doing* to *being*.

From Doing to Being

This whole emphasis on being over doing finds its roots in the teaching of Jesus. While most religions instruct people to *do* certain things to garner favor with God, Christianity is about *being* in relationship with God. In my mind there is no greater call to being in a relationship than in Mark 12:29–31. Here we find Jesus summing up the greatest commandment of all. And it's not at all about a list of things to accomplish to secure a right relationship. It's about *being* . . . in love. Look at what Jesus says when he is asked what the greatest command of all is: "Jesus replied, 'The most important commandment is this: "Listen, O Israel! The LORD our God is the one and only LORD. And you must love the LORD your God with all your heart, all your soul, all your mind, and all your strength." The second is equally important: "Love your neighbor as yourself." No other commandment is greater than these.'"

For me that makes my spirituality very simple: love God and love others. And as I truly love, I come more and more to realize that love is not about a role. It's about a relationship.

There are so many great examples of the relationship emphasis all over the Bible, but none fit so succinctly for this chapter as the story of Martha, Mary, and Jesus. Luke 10 tells us about a scene in which Jesus comes to visit the two sisters, Martha and Mary. In the hustle of getting a big dinner on for Jesus, Martha gets distracted with her to-do list and becomes irritated with Mary, who apparently was no help whatsoever. In verses 38–41 the whole story unfolds, exposing Christ's desire for "*be*-ers" over "*do*-ers."

> As Jesus and the disciples continued on their way to Jerusalem, they came to a certain village where a woman named Martha welcomed him into her home. Her sister, Mary, sat at the Lord's feet, listening to what he taught. But Martha was distracted by the big dinner she was preparing. She came to Jesus and said, "Lord, doesn't it seem unfair to you that my sister just sits here while I do all the work? Tell her to come and help me." But the Lord said to her, "My dear Martha, you are worried and upset over all these details! There is only one thing worth being concerned about. Mary has discovered it, and it will not be taken away from her."

You see, Mary understood the concept of relationship priorities. She knew how to stop, sit, and just *be*, whereas Martha found her greatest drive was to fulfill a role *do*ing. And when Martha could stand no more, wishing to chastise

Mary's apparent laziness, Jesus actually defended Mary's choice, saying in verse 42, "but only one thing is needed. Mary has chosen what is better, and it will not be taken away from her" (NIV).

Now, while I acknowledge that this verse has direct application to *being* over *doing* in our relationship to God, I believe there is another overriding message. In this scene, long ago in a tiny village with these two sisters, I believe Jesus was mandating relationship. I think he was setting a standard for us, communicating not to get so hung up on all the doing stuff in fulfilling a role (such as in mothering) that we fail at loving each other and being in a relationship. It is the crux of what we need to do with our teenagers.

The whole concept of doing and being occurred to me while watching my husband father our son. When I was in the throes of scrambling to find my place and get things in order like Martha—my husband seemed to be making real ground with Will 3 just hanging out—like Mary. He would stay up late, fielding random questions and listening to musings from our son, sometimes until one or two in the morning. Meanwhile I was crashing early so I could rise to get the kids up, make breakfast, and get them out the door. It seemed that while I was busy doing, my husband was busy being. And as I continued managing meals, carpool schedules, and the like, the pulse of my connection with Will 3 seemed to grow faint.

It was breaking my heart, so I decided to try and reengage. Sometimes I would sit and fold laundry while he watched the History Channel, just making myself available should he desire conversation. And I started staying up later at night (which required a catnap almost daily) to catch momentum when he was more motivated to engage. I realized that for some unknown reason those late hours were sacred times for him. They were the times he opened up and was most receptive to deep talks and life reflections. So I prioritized them.

I have to say that a change didn't happen overnight and I still had my Martha moments with him, but slowly I began to see that I had inadvertently bulldozed ahead with my mothering duties and narrowly missed deepening the relationship with my teenager. I had to stop and renegotiate the way I interacted with Will 3 as a young man in the making and ensure that I didn't plow over the important parts of being with him in my effort to be a "good mom" and fly through the checklist for my busy family.

Just Be It

With all the parenting advice floating around out there, just *being* is probably the least doable on paper. Not because of desire, mind you, but because it is one of those incredibly ambiguous things to figure out. If we, as mothers, could craft the perfect moments to enrich the relationship, then no doubt we would do it. It would read just like a how-to article out of *Real Simple* magazine. But being in a relationship is just not that easy—especially with a teenager who could be driving you absolutely nuts.

As a matter of fact, it happened to me just this morning. My girls, Emily (18) and Sara (14), are in the middle of finishing finals this week. And so their schedule is extra screwy. The one thing I remember when I crawled into bed last night was telling Sara that she was in charge of texting her friends to find out what time she needed to be at school for her choir final. The choir final was actually a "choir tour" that consisted of boarding a chartered bus and traveling to various locations around town to sing Christmas carols. The whole tour thing sounded like a great idea, except somehow the Davises managed to miss some pertinent information, like what time the bus was leaving the school parking lot. So my instructions to Sara—to find out what time the bus leaves the parking lot—were of great importance.

Well, when I awoke this morning to realize that Sara couldn't find a single friend who knew the hour of departure, I felt irritated. How could I drive her to school on time if she had no particular idea when she should be there? Oh well, I thought . . . ask another mother. So I emailed and found consensus that the desired arrival was eight sharp. So Sara piled in the car at seven thirty and we headed out to school so she could meet the bus in the parking lot on time.

Now don't ask me how I managed to get going on this, but for some reason, about halfway to school I started a harmless little lecture. I began by illuminating why Sara needed to know her own schedule during finals week (it's not *my* schedule—I am long past the eighth grade). I then pointed out that she should be mature enough to find out when important things, like choir tour finals, take place in her life (or else she will miss the event and make a poor grade). And finally, I asked for the umpteenth time that she give me some advance notice about when and where she needs to be when I am her designated driver (because it is discourteous to assume that any person sits around at another's beck and call). As I drove and discussed (with her occasional "Uh-huh" and "I'm sorry, Mom."), I quickly escalated and uttered a bland but inexcusable expletive. What a great way to nurture the relationship!

You see, what happens in my life is that the test of *being* is mixed in with all the whatnot of real living and obligatory *doing*. And for me, it's so much messier than just making a plan to nurture the relationship. But the gloriously freeing thing here is that even blunders like mine become a part of building a relational bond when handled the way God asks me to. In this case, I did. I immediately understood my mistake and pulled the car over right there on the side of the road to actually talk to Sara instead of lecture her. I told her that I was sorry for my outburst and that it was completely uncalled for. And while I did ask (kindly) that in the future she work on getting more organized in her schedule, I promised that I wouldn't allow my irritation to get in the way of our relationship. I explained that frustration has a way of weaseling in and wrecking us, but that I was determined that it wouldn't impact who we are or who we will be. I prayed with her, asking God and Sara to forgive me, right there in the car. Then I hugged her and she laughed because it was kinda funny when I said what I said—though not particularly charming. But mostly, I think she laughed because we

> Grace is the light or electricity or juice or breeze that takes you from that isolated place and puts you with others who are as startled and embarrassed and eventually grateful as you are to be there.[3]
>
> Anne Lamott,
> *Traveling Mercies*

were still okay. She realized that when she's not on her game, we're okay. And when I'm not on my game, we're going to be okay. Because deep inside we both know that it's not getting to a final on time or having a perfect mom that cements the relationship—it's just us, together, at whatever place we're at that keeps things right. Me and Sara.

Take a Deep Breath

So put down that day planner, shove aside your perceptions of what a perfect mother looks like, and take a deep breath. What your teenager really needs is you. Period. That's the you who tries hard and messes up, the one who is sometimes on her game and sometimes not. It's you just being you. Not the accomplished Martha mom but the accessible Mary mom. That's *the* necessary ingredient for raising your teenager.

PARENTING YOUR TEEN

- What is your specific strategy for raising your teenager? If you haven't formulated one, what would you identify as a de facto plan already in place?
- Where are you in regard to *doing* (role) and *being* (relationship) with your teenager? How might a shift from *doing* to *being* affect your relationship?
- Why do you think that ongoing *doing* from Mom often irritates preteens and teens? What might your *doing* be communicating?

- Honest answer: Does your teenager routinely hurt your feelings? Is there a chance that there is some unresolved bitterness on your part toward your teen because of a shift in the relationship?

- Are you more of a Martha mom or a Mary mom? Explain.

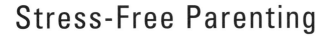

Stress-Free Parenting

From Fear to Faith

Parental anxiety is at an all-time high—and especially to-night! It's New Year's Eve and I have teenagers . . . need I say more? My eighteen-year-old daughter headed out the door a couple of hours ago to a friend's house. *Safe enough*, I think to myself—but she doesn't want to stay the night, so she's driving home after midnight—*not safe enough*, I retort. And my son (who is home visiting during Christmas break) has just left our house at 8 p.m. to drive to a New Year's Eve party in another city some three hours away with several of his fraternity brothers—all of whom are legally able to have a celebratory drink and ring in the new year. When I sent them out the door with a hug, a kiss, and a motherly, "Be careful out there tonight—you know there are going to be all kinds of people drinking and driving . . . ," they both suppressed a smile, nodded their heads in agreement, and tried to look mindful. They don't worry about things like drunkards roaming the roads, because they, like most adolescents, suffer psychosis about their invincibility. And this brazen confidence nearly drives me, their dear mother, crazy.

My kids don't understand my apprehension—and they don't make a habit of paying attention to negative statistics involving young people of their age. Like the report that motor vehicle crashes are the leading cause of death among American teenagers, killing between 5,000 and 6,000 teenagers every year, and that "no other kind of hazard comes close to claiming as many teenage lives."[1] Those statistics. The ones that linger in my mind when my kids wander out the door.

And it's not just the driving that triggers this anxiety; there's oh so much more to think about as the mother of teenagers. I've gathered just a few of the more startling statistics from various national studies as reported by SADD (Students Against Destructive Decisions at www.sadd.org). Are you ready?

- About two-fifths of students (41%) have consumed alcohol (more than just a few sips) by 8th grade.
- More than half (58%) of 12th graders report having been drunk at least once in their life. One-fifth (20%) of 8th graders report having been drunk at least once in their life.
- Nationwide, 25.4% of students had been offered, sold, or given an illegal drug by someone on school property during the 12 months preceding the survey.

- Half of teens (50%) have tried an illicit drug by the time they finish high school.
- Currently [2005 report] 46.8% of all high school students report they have had sexual intercourse.
- The majority of both girls and boys who are sexually active wish they had waited. Of those who have had sex, more than one-half of teen boys (55%) and the majority of teen girls (70%) said they wish they had waited longer to have sex.
- Nineteen (19) million new STD infections occur each year, almost half of them among young people ages 15 to 24.[2]

Scared? It certainly freaks me out. Apparently, many parents feel the same way, and that in effect has created a parenting philosophy that is reactive instead of proactive. A philosophy driven by an excessive, yet culturally excusable paranoia instead of peace. And the paranoid mindset is driven deep into our collective mothering soul every time we read the paper or watch the news. Or many times it's embedded when we hear the latest heartbreak—whether it's a teen on his way to rehab for Adderall abuse or a high school girl who just found out she's pregnant. The stories are all there, threatening us into some sort of action.

If we're really honest, we must admit that it isn't just about protecting kids from sexually transmitted diseases or illicit drug use. If we're truthful, we have to admit it has mushroomed to include other problems as well, whether social, academic, or extracurricular. Like the mom who goes to great pains to protect her daughter from petty girl politics, or the parents who set up a meeting with the teacher to discuss their teen's C in biology, or the dad who confronts the basketball coach about "equal playing time" for his son.

We want our teens to have the kind of life that we envision will make them happy, well adjusted, and successful. We don't want our kids' oversights to wreck their lives—the lapses like gossiping and instigating the girl politics, or blowing off the biology final and barely securing a passing grade, or warming the bench an entire basketball season because "it's just not worth the hustle." We don't want them suffering those kinds of consequences; they are too painful to endure.

In addition to the consequences associated with poor decision making, there are other hardships that are a standard part of living in a teenage world, like the fact that the world revolves around the prettiest, the fastest, and the smartest—and that it has since the dawn of the age. That's not fair. And so if padding the fall or leveling the playing field just a smidge helps our kids get ahead, so be it. I know that's how I often feel—if there is something I can do as a parent to prevent the pain associated with poor decision making, teenaged injustice, or just plain teen foolishness, show me the way.

Patterns of Critically Concerned Parents

Though this idea of protecting kids whatever the cost is somewhat of an unrealistic goal, American parents everywhere are still reaching for it. In the late '90s, authors Foster Cline and Jim Fay of *Parenting with Love and Logic* recognized growing behavior patterns among critically concerned parents and termed several labels to identify them.[3] One of these labels coined by Cline and Fay is the *drill sergeant*. Drill sergeant parents are the ones who completely micro-

"There are a lot of things I can't control," said one Bethesda mother who asked not to be identified because, she said, her daughter would be mortified. "Terrorists, the environment. But I can control how my daughter spends her day."[4]

Valerie Strauss, "Putting Parents
in Their Place: Outside Class"

manage their kids' lives by providing absolutes with few if any options by dictating how their children should act, react, and feel about personal issues and choices. In other words, they're controllers. The second group of parents identified by the authors were labeled the *helicopter parent*. These parents want to let go and allow for a child's autonomy yet have real difficulty, and instead stick very close to their children, hovering overhead, ready to swoop in and fix things, thereby disallowing any negativity. In other words, they're worrier/fixers.

So what's wrong with a little controlling/worrying/fixing in regard to your teenager? Actually, quite a lot. When parents rush in, they are not only hindering independent growth, but they are also communicating an extremely negative message: *You can't handle life without me.* Now, while that might exemplify exactly how a mother truly feels about her teen, it is absolutely the most injurious message she can send. What we fail to keep in mind as mothers, especially when that kid is needy and pulling on our heartstrings, is this: The goal is *independence.* The goal is *separation. Our ultimate goal, as a mother, is to work ourselves right out of a job.*

While that might seem especially harsh, continually ignoring the end goal of a healthy separation puts a teenager in an extremely unstable place psychologically. As a matter of fact, university administrators nationwide have noted an alarming trend with incoming freshman students—the tendency for these students to have abnormally overinvolved parents. Helen Johnson, a consultant on parent relations for some of America's top universities and coauthor of the book *Don't Tell Me What to Do, Just Send Money*, believes the parent overinvolvement problem is rampant, even at the college level, and it's creating a crisis on campus.[5] What is the crisis? Emotionally fragile students. Overzealous parents (aka "helicopter parents") are raising overdependent teenagers, and they are leaving home as fragile young adults. *Psychology Today*'s Hara Estroff Marano, in an article entitled "A Nation of Wimps," explains it this way:

> No one doubts that there are significant economic forces pushing parents to invest so heavily in their children's outcome from an early age. But taking all the discomfort, disappointment and even the play out of development, especially while increasing pressure for success, turns out to be misguided by just about 180 degrees. With few challenges all their own, kids are unable to forge their creative adaptations to the normal vicissitudes of life. That not only makes them risk-averse, it makes them psychologically fragile, riddled with anxiety. In the process they're robbed of identity, meaning and a sense of accomplishment, to say nothing of a shot at real happiness. Forget, too, about perseverance, not simply a moral virtue but a necessary life skill. These turn out to be the spreading psychic fault lines of 21st-century youth.

Whether we want to or not, we're on our way to creating a nation of wimps.

College, it seems, is where the fragility factor is now making its greatest mark. It's where intellectual and developmental tracks converge as the emotional training wheels come off. By all accounts, psychological distress is rampant on college campuses. It takes a variety of forms, including anxiety and depression—which are increasingly regarded as two faces of the same coin—binge drinking and substance abuse, self-mutilation and other forms of disconnection. The mental state of students is now so precarious for so many that, says Steven Hyman, provost of Harvard University and former director of the National Institute of Mental Health, "it is interfering with the core mission of the university."[6]

Yikes! Is Mr. Hyman actually saying that a parent's well-meaning intentions to protect, help, and guide a teenager could result in not only developing a fragile individual but that the collective effort by parents nationwide could also actually interfere with something as monumental as the core mission of the Harvard University?!? My, oh my. Something's got to change.

> Every fall, parents drop off their well-groomed freshmen and within two or three days many have consumed a dangerous amount of alcohol and placed themselves in harm's way. These kids have been controlled for so long, they just go crazy.[7]
>
> John Portmann, professor of religious studies at the University of Virginia

New Parenting Patterns

It concerns me to think we are raising a nation of wimps, kids who deal with stress in life by binge drinking, substance abuse, or staying connected in an unhealthy parental relationship—emotional umbilical cord attached directly to Mommy. I want neither. But the problem is, I can easily identify myself as a "helicopter–drill sergeant" parent through various stages of raising my kids. Maybe you can too. So what's a mom to do?

The key is creating a parenting pattern that is healthy for your teenager, one that is designed for the ultimate goal of autonomy. You did this when your kids were learning to walk. As a mother, you held them steady while they wobbled out those first steps, but eventually you let go. And when you finally released those tiny chubby hands, you knew there would be times that your sweet baby pumpkin would fall and bump her head. But you also instinctively knew that if you didn't allow for some bumps and bruises in the process, your baby would never learn to toddle. It's the same in parenting a teenager—but the statistical bumps and bruises are so much scarier. And that's the reality that has you, me, and so many other parents freaking out.

We're afraid—that's the thing. It's fear that creates a frantic feeling to hypercontrol, and it's fear that creates an overwhelming sense of anxiety. And while I *highly* recommend Cline and Fay's book *Love and Logic* (the tools are invaluable), knowing how to disengage from destructive parenting practices will not solve your problems, but addressing the root cause of fear itself will. The only way to get over the inherent fear in rearing teenagers through adolescence—

and the destructive parenting practices therein—is to ground yourself in a faith greater than your skill and greater than your teenager's ability to make wise choices. *We must hold fast to a parenting pattern grounded in faith instead of fear.*

> Children . . . are not the only ones who are harmed by hyperconcern. Vigilance is enormously taxing—and it's taken all the fun out of parenting.[8]
>
> Hara Estroff Marano,
> "A Nation of Wimps"

For me, that means that I need to be extremely dependent upon God. I need a relationship with him that is so tight and fast that my impulse in parenting is to lean into his knowledge and his care for my teenager, not into those scary statistics. And I must remember that while I birthed and have the privilege of raising these precious children in my house, they are first and foremost God's, not mine.

See, I don't own my kids, and neither do you—we are stewards. Stewards are people who manage things for someone else. And in this case, we are managing these amazing kids for God. He has gifted you with these children for a season. And he doesn't just hope that you'll try real hard or do whatever sounds best; instead, God expects you and me to view parenting as a mission straight from him. And he expects us to parent according to his wisdom.

As a steward, I understand and act upon the knowledge that God holds my teenager in his hands. I believe that he will not allow my teen to be tempted beyond what she is able to handle. And though I may have great aspirations for her life, I realize that those dreams might not be God's best plans, so I submit myself to God and his leadership, appreciating that he will lead her in his ways, not my ways. And as hard as it is for me to even type, I realize that some of his ways will include adversity and loneliness and complexity and heartache. (Whimper . . .)

Faith says, "I believe in what God has planned for my teenager. I will help her manage it all: the good and the bad." Fear says, "I will protect my teenager from all the things that might harm her. I will continually mother and manage her to keep her safe from all things dangerous."

Understanding the Roots of Faithless Parenting

Faith doesn't come easy to me, especially in regard to parenting. But what I have realized is that it's not because God isn't able; it's because I have trust issues with God. Many of my trust issues stem from my childhood experiences.

At fourteen, I witnessed a murder in my eighth grade classroom—a student shot and killed my teacher with a rifle point blank in front of me and thirty other classmates. In addition, my best friend's sister was raped, her neck sliced open, then she was tied to a tree and left for dead. My neighbor's stepmother was brutally attacked with a screwdriver by a deranged vagrant hiding in her attic. These experiences and others have etched a stronghold of unimaginable fear in my psyche. And though I dealt with many of the repercussions as a young adult, when I became a mother, they all took on a new and devastating meaning. It was one thing for me to witness violent crime, but God forbid my children should ever go through what those people went through. And God forbid I should experience that sort of pain on my child's behalf. Those are the kinds of thoughts that drive me to parent from a place of fear and not of faith.

What I have found is that often my inability to parent out of a faith perspective is really about pain avoidance. For example, when my kids left for their respective New Year's Eve parties, my thought was, "That's not safe . . . late night driving . . . drunk drivers on the road." My conditioned response was one of "don't let bad things happen," which has a lot to do with what I witnessed in junior high. But if I could dig even deeper and examine my true inner response, I would hear a voice screaming like a little baby inside my heart, "No! Don't do it—it makes me so scared. Please stop making me feel so scared. I don't want anything bad to ever happen again." Just being honest. My desire to manage and control my kids, instead of believing God for them, has a lot to do with avoiding pain: theirs and mine. And in listening to other mothers, I see the same thing with them too.

Like my friend Lisa. Her daughter Jenny is seventeen, precocious, and looks like a model for Victoria's Secret. (She actually looks a lot like her mother did when she was her age.) The thing is, Lisa is terrified that Jenny will "go over the line" where boys are concerned. She accelerates into hyperdrive when Jenny is with boys—whether they are just friends or guys that Jenny likes and wants to date. But because she is so vigilant about protecting Jenny's purity, Lisa often lapses into lecturing her even when she is around her friends—embarrassing and demeaning Jenny. Though Lisa has trouble realizing it, her manic attention is a result of negative consequences in her own life. When Lisa was a teenager, she not only had sex but also ended up getting pregnant and having an abortion. Lisa plainly doesn't want

Jenny to live with the same remorse and the shame and the painful memories. So Lisa focuses on the statistics, attempting to scare Jenny into compliance regarding her sexuality. And as Lisa allows fear to be her primary parenting focus, Jenny pushes away. Moving further and further down the road of sexual experimentation.

So what's the point? Am I asking you to be fearless? To ignore your past regardless of it's impact? To mask your real feelings? No, I am asking you to realize a very important truth: God is in control, and he is big enough to handle your teenager's worst choices, their biggest temptations, and even protect them from things you don't know how to handle. And all the effort in the world cannot protect and guide your teenager the way God can, so I implore you to beg God for help and direction. To put aside fear and parent instead with a complete faith in God.

Psalm 127:1 says this: "Unless the LORD builds the house, its builders labor in vain. Unless the LORD watches over the city, the watchmen stand guard in vain" (NIV). It could be rephrased for parents, "Unless the Lord raises the teenager, her parents labor in vain. Unless the Lord watches over the teenager, the parents stand guard in vain." As mothers, we must acknowledge that even our best-laid plans will fail without God. Unless he is in the business of building and securing our teenager's life, all our hard work will be in vain. He alone is their builder and their keeper.

Stress-Free Parenting from the Father's Point of View

While parenting teens will never be completely stress free, there are some incredible benefits from trusting God to "build the house." When you honestly examine the foundation of your life—as in where you place your confidence and trust—and then allow God to provide the proper impetus for parenting, the job can actually be a joyful endeavor. And when you do experience fears, the best thing you can do is be honest with God and your teenager. For me, that looks like praying and asking God for the courage to "smile at the future" when I consider my teenagers (Prov. 31:25). I also pray for "faithful instruction" and "wisdom" when I talk to my kids (Prov. 31:26). And in the times that I feel myself seize up in apprehension over one of their decisions, I ask God to "help me overcome my unbelief" (Mark 9:23) about his goodness and ability to "build the house."

There is another thing I do that I think enriches my relationship with my teenagers more than any other. I let my teenagers in on my journey of trusting God. It's so important that teenagers see how you struggle to trust God in difficult times—and parenting is no exception. All three of my kids know that I have some trigger trusting points. They know my history. And if I freak out about something, they have an understanding of why I act the way I do. I have been honest about my resistance to trust God in regard to "bad things happening," and in doing so, I have revealed myself to them as a fellow Christ follower. I am not just their mother; I am a human being wrestling through faith issues—just like them.

These are the years to let your teen see you as a sister in Christ as well as a mother. Let your teenager peek in at your frail human heart and see how God makes himself strong in you as you work through all these things together. And pray together for each other—two people who share the same hope, the same faith, and the same heavenly Father.

PARENTING YOUR TEEN

- Which of the SADD statistics make you especially impassioned or even angry?
- What is your greatest fear for your teenager? (If you have more than one child, list your fears for each child.)
- How are your fears motivating and directing some of your parenting decisions? Is there a chance that your teenagers are in some ways prisoners of your own fear?
- How might your fears communicate to your teenager that she can't make it on her own?
- List the differences between ownership and stewardship. How does the inherent mindset affect how you handle situations with your teenager?
- Is there a chance that your fears about your kids are actually self-realized in your own life? How might imposing fear on your children act as a self-fulfilling prophecy?
- How will allowing your teenager to see your struggles with God heighten his maturity and sensitivity to spiritual things? How will it impact his ability to trust God?

Section Two

A Practical
MOM

*~ actively engaged
in some course of action ~*

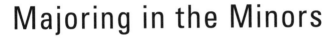

Majoring in the Minors

Keeping a Level Head about Your Expectations

A couple years back in a moment of pure naiveté, I offered to take care of ten Labrador puppies. My sister and her family planned a ski vacation to Crested Butte, and since she invited my teenage son to go along, I felt it was only fair to offer to keep her puppies at my house while they were gone. It seemed like a fair swap. Besides, someone needed to watch all those puppies, so I figured, why not me? I love puppies. They are so cuddly and cute—I figured caring for the darlings would be a piece of cake.

When my sister brought over the wiggling bunch of babies, they were small. The puppies had just been weaned, and I received specific instructions about how much to feed them and how to ensure that their living space was clean and healthy.

Now at this point, they seemed irresistible. They even had that oh-so-awesome puppy smell clinging to their yellow fuzzy coats. The thought of mothering this furry brood was exciting. So I set up a small play place and sleeping pad for the puppies in a sectioned portion of our garage.

The first day was dreamy. The precious little things slept most the day away. They were worn out from the exhausting trip to their new home and quietly piled in a corner, a mass of sleeping beauties. But something unexpected happened the next morning. We were awakened *very early* by a pack of yapping dogs. My husband and I rushed out to the garage to begin the arduous job of feeding and soothing the frantic beasts. They seemed to have doubled in size overnight! But there was something else that needed attention . . . the job of cleaning up after the dirty darlings.

See, puppies do three things really well—eat, sleep, and poop. And they don't seem to be particularly discerning about where they do any of those things in relation to the other, if you know what I mean.

This went on for several days, and ever the conscientious surrogate mother, I dutifully tried to maintain a sterile environment for the litter. Clothed with gloves and armed with cleaner, I felt if I was diligent enough, I could keep them from traipsing around in their own untidiness. Of course this was an insane goal but one I clung to religiously. Cleanliness is next to godliness, after all!

Well, as you can imagine, my life quickly became a cesspool of soiled newspaper, disinfectant, and dirty paws. By day five, I was a smidge . . . shall we say . . . over the edge. I vividly remember standing in the garage with puppies jumping on my legs, their wet paws smearing my jeans. I cried out to my husband, sobbing my eyes out because I just couldn't get things cleaned up fast enough. My husband rushed in to find me hysterical, pleading for help. He looked at the puppies and he looked up at me. Then he took me by the shoulders, gave me a firm shake, and exclaimed, *"Susie! It's just dog poop!!"*

A Smidge over the Edge

Though in the beginning my goals were innocent enough, I lost complete perspective on reality while caring for those puppies. Let's get real . . . did I think that I could keep ten yellow puppies from squishing around in their own poop? Yes, for a few frantic days I did. But you know what? What started out exciting quickly became exhausting because I was making a really big deal about something inconsequential and unavoidable. Puppies will play around in their own poop. I know it's gross but it's just one of those things you have to expect when puppies are little and undignified.

> The art of being wise is the art of knowing what to overlook.
>
> William James

I think we often do the same with our teenagers. As mothers, we get whirled up in a completely asinine assignment, like thinking that teenagers must keep a completely spotless room, and then we fall apart when they fail to meet our goals. We start majoring in the minors, and the relationship becomes a cesspool of soiled expectations. Is it *that* big a deal for a kid to leave a pair of nasty, blackened athletic socks on the floor? I agree it's really gross, but freaking out about it isn't the best way to handle that kind of poop.

As mothers of teenagers, job numero uno is keeping a balanced and reasonable perspective about our expectations. It's the ability to keep an appropriate outlook on adolescence that allows us to go with the flow—and keep our mouths quiet—when we feel as though our teens aren't quite measuring up. Because if we don't, we could end up raising some sick little puppies.

Lesson in the Lunchroom

Whenever I get a little whacked out, distressed that my teenagers aren't living up to my expectations, I remember to give myself an imaginary shoulder shake from the biblical writer Solomon. Ecclesiastes 7:13 says, "Accept the way God does things, for who can straighten what he has made crooked?" Let's apply that to parenting teens. Now I am not insinuating that teenagers are crooked in a negative, twisted way, but teenagers have a bend, if you will, and all the micromanaging in the world will not unbend them.

I was reminded of this last week when I visited my youngest at her junior high school. It was Sara's fourteenth birthday and I had promised to bring her a meal from Sonic. I handed her the coveted bag of fast food and settled in to enjoy visiting with her and her friends.

I couldn't have been there more than a few minutes when I noticed some striking similarities among the girls. First, all these precious seventh grade girls were excitedly eating and talking at the same time. I noticed, of course, because it is one of my pet peeves. I harp continually on Sara at our dinner table at home about talking with food in her mouth. She gets so excited that when a thought pops into her head that she wants to share, the mouth starts rolling without regard to the food inside. The second thing I noticed at the cafeteria table is that the girls all got up and down a lot. In midbite, a girl would dart to another table and talk to a friend, then come back and pick up the pizza where she left off. I've seen this at home before too. Sitting there at the lunchroom table was quite eye opening. A lesson in child development.

What I realized (again) is that too often I cocoon up at home with my family and forget about regular teenage development. I forget that Sara is just about where other fourteen-years-olds are as far as etiquette is concerned. She's really pretty normal. And it reminds me not to push too hard at the dinner table when she gets excited about saying something even if she has food in her mouth. Or if she jumps up from the table without excusing herself. Does that mean that I won't gently and sensitively remind her about her table manners? Of course not. That's my job. But I need to be careful and not communicate that it's a life-and-death situation should she speak with food in her mouth.

Teenagers are growing, and there are particular teenage bends or curves that we as mothers must become familiar with. As a matter of fact, for every age of a teenager's life, there are "average" milestones, just like when they were infants. In the same way a toddler can be expected to throw green peas to the floor in disgust, a teenager can be expected to do a little eye rolling when you ask them to clean their room. Pretty normal. Toddlers are exhausting, teens are testy. And if you happen to have a teenager that dutifully cleans her room with nary a roll of the eyes, be grateful!

The important thing here, Mom, is to *know* what's normal developmentally and to handle the difference between your expectations and your teen's healthy development with wisdom. Don't let the gulf get too wide, because that's when you are at great risk of exasperating your teenager—and wrecking your relationship.

What Is "Pretty Normal" Anyway?

Growing up, my dad always quipped that his goal for us kids was that we would turn out "*pretty* normal." He said this because he realized that no family is 100 percent completely normal and that "normal" is an incredibly difficult standard to quantify. So when one of us did something particularly screwy, my dad tended to exhibit grace if he felt we were still hitting the mark in "pretty normal" range.

It's important to have the ability to differentiate what "normal" teenage development looks like. As a mother, it's crucial to determine where your teenager is in their physical, emotional, mental, and spiritual development so that you won't have unrealistic expectations and risk overreacting.

So what is normal for your teenager? While I can't begin to pinpoint exact behavior as normal or abnormal in the constraints of this chapter, I will alert you to groundbreaking research in the area of adolescent development that will enable you to understand more of what's going on in their minds. In her book *The Primal Teen: What the New Discoveries about the Teenage Brain Tell Us about Our Kids*, author Barbara Strauch reveals that, though scientists at one point thought that the teenage brain was completely developed like an adult's brain, that is far from the truth. Neuroscientists have in fact found that the teenage brain is still under construction and that the "changes taking place in the brain during adolescence are so profound, they may rival early childhood as a critical period of development. The teenage brain, far from being ready-made, undergoes a surprisingly complex and crucial development."[1]

So yes, that does in essence mean you have a sixteen-year-old, 6'2", two-hundred-pound teenage "toddler" running around—which might account for the fact that he can't really explain why he made the decision to roll through the stop sign even as you were sitting next to him in the front seat. While your teenagers may have you dumbfounded by their behavior, in a sense, they're a little confused by it too. And there's actually a reason for that confusion. Strauch explains further, "The teenage brain, it's now becoming clear, is still very much a work in progress, a giant construction project. Millions of connections are being hooked up; millions more are swept away. Neurochemicals wash over the teenage brain, giving it a new paint job, a new look, a new chance at life. The teenage brain is raw, vulnerable. It's a brain that's still becoming what it will be."[2]

Scientists seem to agree that it's the "becoming" phase that makes teens look, act, and sound . . . well, kinda crazy. In other words, kinda crazy is *pretty normal* for teenagers.

For me, that research evidence means that I shouldn't expect perfection. That I can count on some "terrible two"-type tantrums. That there is a possibility that I should believe my teenager when he says he "just forgot" to study for a history test. And that sometimes I should bite my tongue when my distracted daughter needs a third reminder to feed the dogs. I might be wise to remember that it's all pretty normal.

Primarily, I think the research points us in the direction of making sure we are gracious about what they're going through. To remember that while we might have certain expectations, we shouldn't get to the point with our teenagers where the expectations end up exasperating them.

Keeping Unrealistic Expectations from Exasperating Your Teenager

It's tricky to balance between expectation and exaspera-tion. As a parent, you likely have certain standards for your teenager, and rightly so. But if the demands for achieving the standard are beyond the capacity to deliver, you could have an angry or depressed kid on your hands. *Exasperation* is defined as causing irritation or annoyance or exciting to anger. And here you might be thinking, "Yes! Exactly. My teenager is exasperating me!" And while that may be true, the onus for keeping anger from setting into family life is on the parents, not the teenagers. Not only that, it's actually presented in the Bible as a command. Ephesians 6:4 says, "Do not irritate and provoke your children to anger [do not exasperate them to resentment], but rear them [tenderly] in the training and discipline and the counsel and admonition of the Lord" (AMP). Another translation says it like this: "Parents, don't be hard on your children. Raise them properly. Teach them and instruct them about the Lord" (CEV).

The way I see it, the verse is broken down into three simple parts. First, we must not be too

> The teenage brain may, in fact, be briefly insane. But, scientists say, it is crazy by design. The teenage brain is in flux, maddening and muddled. And that's how it's supposed to be.[3]
>
> Barbara Strauch,
> *The Primal Teen*

hard on our kids. In other words, it's our job to be aware of what pretty normal looks like for every teenager in our family and to act or react accordingly. Because it's only then that we can keep from pushing them over the edge. Second, we have a responsibility to raise them properly. I view that as the green light for teaching them about manners and whatnot. Just because our teenagers are still "under construction" doesn't mean that we just let everything slide. Likewise, we shouldn't let the research deceive us into thinking that we must maintain toddler expectations for a teenager. They still need to be reminded how to treat people or about basic social graces. And finally, we must be committed to developing them spiritually. This is extremely difficult to do if there is undue strain and tension in the relationship. The capacity to train a teenager spiritually is granted in a good relationship. In truth, our ability to be an encourager instead of an exasperator is directly linked to keeping a level head and having reasonable expectations, because if there is anger and resentment in the relationship, it's not likely that there will be much spiritual development going on at all.

Being a Balanced Mom

Achieving balance need not be an exhausting endeavor. It just takes some careful observation and some insight from God above. Get in the habit of taking notes (mentally, *pleeeeze!*) when you are around other teens, and later pray for wisdom about your expectations with your own teen. Honestly assess your relationship with your teenager and ask God for guidance in narrowing the gap between what you want and what he wants for your child. Though it might seem difficult in the beginning, the end result is appreciation. For your teen—and from your teen.

■ ■ ■ ■ ■ ■ ■ ■ ■

PARENTING YOUR TEEN

- List some typical "bends" of teenage development. (For example, moodiness, increasing preference for time spent with peers, limited worldview, etc.)
- List some of your expectations for your teenager in these areas: academic, social, emotional, physical, and spiritual.
- Think back to your own teenage years. How likely would you have been as a teenager to meet all of the expectations that you have for your child currently?
- If there is a discrepancy between what you hope for your child and what you actually experienced as a teen, what is the root of your expectation?
- Honestly, how are your expectations affecting your relationship with your teenager? How might this be impacting your potential to be a spiritual guide for your teen?
- What are some practical steps to stop exasperating and start encouraging the relationship?
- How does appreciating the wonder of the development of your teenager's brain affect your ability to stay balanced in your parenting?

Laying Down the Law

Rules for Your Teen's Life

When our first child, Will 3, was born in 1986, we had strict instructions from the pediatrician to tightly swaddle him and be sure to *lay him on his stomach* to sleep. Current research dictated that infants faced the best odds for surviving those fragile early weeks if they were sleeping flat on their tummies. Three years later, Emily came along and the orders from the doctor were the exact opposite: Emily should sleep *flat on her back*. A real surprise to me that expert opinion changed so fast. It seems that the updated research supplied to the specialists included instructing mothers everywhere to lay their swaddled babies face up. Some three and a half years later, our youngest, Sara, was born. And of course, new operating instructions: Sara was swaddled and laid on her side.

Either side, that is, but definitely *on her side*. Apparently that sleeping position gave her the best chance of survival.

I remember diligently following the doctor's orders. I certainly didn't want to risk hurting my child by failing to follow expert opinion. So I dutifully swaddled and laid each child the direction appointed by the doctor. I remember creeping in to check on them as they lay sleeping to make sure my babies were still facing the right direction. Though I didn't understand all the reasoning behind the research—and I was curious that the rules changed every three years—I was dutiful about my babies maintaining their sleeping positions. Down, up, and then on the side.

Operating Instructions for Teenagers

Life seemed a bit easier back then when they were little. You simply followed the doctor's orders, and usually baby developed just fine. But enter adolescence and things change dramatically. Though opinions abound, no one seems to know exactly how to handle the kid entering puberty. While most pediatricians agree that inoculating against childhood illness is paramount to physical health, few could tell you with conviction the way to establish social, emotional, and

> Adolescence begins earlier and lasts longer. Kids live in a far more complex world than their parents did and they are exposed to a lot of stuff before they have the cognitive and emotional faculties to deal with it.[1]
>
> Hara Estroff Marano, "The Campus Crisis"

spiritual health in your teenager's life. It's as if there isn't a documented, failproof plan to inoculate your teen from the inherent hazards facing them. Operating instructions can be somewhat ambiguous, and it seems the only thing experts can agree upon is the fact that it's an incredibly crazy time for teenagers and parents alike.

If you take a straw poll among your friends, it's probable that all will agree that little girls and boys are not only growing bigger and taller than we did at their age but they are also hitting puberty much sooner. Drop your kids off at the local elementary school and you are very likely to see a ten-year-old girl wearing a bra who really needs it. For girls, the years preceding thirteen are the ones when most of the eye-popping change takes place. And though boys are typically slower to develop than girls, their obvious interest in the girls wearing bras indicates that they are actually hitting puberty too.

What's all that mean to you and me? Only that adolescence is starting younger and lasting longer, which in essence means that we are parenting "teenagers" more years on the whole. Think of it this way: if your child begins puberty at ten and doesn't finish maturing emotionally until, say, twenty-one, you could be parenting someone with a teenager's psyche for over a decade. Whew.

With that in mind, it's easy to understand why parenting a teenager is so demanding. It lasts such a long time—much longer than the terrible twos. And while we can phone a pediatrician for questions regarding physical health or ask a teacher at school about academic milestones, it seems we're at a loss about how to handle those everyday problems that come up, like how to handle your emotional preteen when she comes home crying because she's *the only one in the whole school* who doesn't have a cell phone. Or maybe when your son just called to tell you he had *another fender bender* and he's only had his driver's license six months. Where's the expert advice for that kind of stuff?

The Law and the Rules

While I have yet to find the "all-encompassing, authoritative, last book you'll ever need to read on raising teenagers," there is something all-important that every mother needs to know regarding operating instructions for her teenager: *the difference between the law and the rules.*

The *law* is what I would use to describe as the absolutes for a child's life—and in the case of a teenager, those absolutes would include any and all existing laws created by our government, such as "children under twenty-one do not drink alcohol." Laws seem fairly universal, and gratefully, most parents are in wholehearted agreement in identifying them and requiring compliance in their teenagers. Not many parents encourage teens to smoke, do drugs, drink alcohol, or make the kinds of irrational decisions that inherently hurt themselves or others. The parents who do promote teens to engage in such behavior are the ones most likely to end up on *The Maury Show*.

But there is another part of the law too, and it impacts parents whether they are spiritually minded or not. That law is the abiding standards set by God to define morality. Non-Christian and Christian families alike tend to recognize and appreciate these laws. They include instructions like abstaining from premarital sex, being truthful, and honoring

> Adulthood no longer begins when adolescence ends, according to a recent report by University of Pennsylvania sociologist Frank F. Furstenberg and colleagues. There is, instead, a growing no-man's-land of postadolescence from 20 to 30, which they dub "early adulthood." Those in it look like adults but "haven't become fully adult yet—traditionally defined as finishing school, landing a job with benefits, marrying and parenting—because they are not ready or perhaps not permitted to do so.[2]
>
> Hara Estroff Marano, "A Nation of Wimps"

your father and mother. Most parents, whether they say so or not, hope for their kids to become teenagers of character with the kinds of values that are set forth in the Bible.

So in essence the law consists of the law of man and the law of God. (And actually, many of our national laws are derived from the laws found in the Bible.)

But honestly, the law isn't typically the area where parents have trouble knowing how to handle their teenagers. Parents usually feel they are on firm footing when requiring kids to comply with the law. But the *rules* . . . that's a whole different story. The rules reside in that murky gray area where parents have to guide their children with excruciating detail, and those are the areas that seem to trip most parents up. The rules are the individual family guidelines that kids seriously balk at when entering their teens. Because unlike the law, many times the rules cannot be found in the annals of law books at the capitol or even in the pages of the Bible. The rules are more subjective. They are established by parents for kids to follow—or more honestly restated, they are established by parents for teenagers to challenge. Rules are things like if and when teens will have full access to driving a car, or whether or not they are permitted to go to a sleepover where both boys and girls are staying all night (ahem). Or when they'll car date, or if they should be required to keep their room spotless. It's the rules that make the water both murky and turbulent in the life of a teenager and her mom.

Ruling the Gray Matter

Over the past couple of days, I talked with two mom friends who are dealing with this very problem: establishing life rules for their kids. One was completely startled and caught off guard by a situation that arose with her preteen (age twelve) son. He and his buddies hatched a fabulous idea to take their "girlfriends" to a movie—without a chaperone. All the other parents seemed fine with the arrangement, but my friend Jan felt in her gut it was the wrong decision for her son. She was hoping Bryan would put off "dating" for much, much later. And she just couldn't believe that she was facing what she long dreaded—the whole "girl" thing. It's not that she minded his attraction to those cute girls in his class, but to jump-start the whole thing with a movie date . . . she could just imagine it—dark theater, sitting side by side, boy slides his arm up over girl's shoulder, then starts stealing sideways glances for the *perfect moment . . . to get a first kiss*! No, not at twelve . . . absolutely not!

My friend Jill had a completely different situation. Her tenth-grade daughter, Ashley, came home with what Jill considered an extremely skimpy swimsuit. Apparently, Ashley and her friends made a trip to the mall, where they all helped each find flattering swimsuits, and while Jill had no idea what the other suits looked like, she felt Ashley's just didn't do enough to cover her daughter's birthday suit. The minute Jill saw the tiny yellow thing, she expressly prohibited Ashley from wearing it. It infuriated Ashley that her mother didn't "trust her" to "pick out a stupid swimsuit!" when, according to Ashley, the other mothers barely breathed a peep about the skimpy factor. Attempting a compromise, Jill offered to buy her another suit, but Ashley was so outraged she wouldn't even speak to her mother about the situation. She stomped off to her room and slammed the door behind her.

If you're a parent of a preteen or teenager, you have likely stumbled on situations just like these. You see the problem, analyze it (often agonize over it), and come up with a rule based on your best wisdom. Then to your surprise, your teen swirls up into a storm of emotionalism, challenging every piece of your parenting prowess. It's as if, during those scant months of development between child and teen, you have magically morphed from an all-knowing, wise benefactor into a completely pitiful excuse for a parent—someone who has no idea how to create livable rules. And while you might be able to hold firm on the decision (especially if you have reinforcement from dad), on the inside there is a torrent of misgiving, leading you down the lonely path of apprehension.

It's overwhelming when you get to that breaking point, feeling like you have absolutely no idea what you're doing and secretly wondering if maybe your parenting (and all those unique family rules) are actually hurting your teens instead of helping them. And it's those gray areas that seem to stir up the most insecurity. Because where once you had a battalion of reinforcements in the form of your like-minded friends parenting kids of similar age, all the like-mindedness seems to have disappeared. Your best friend who has a girl your daughter's age is actually letting her daughter keep her string bikini because, as your friend put it, "They have to start making their own decisions sometime." And your neighbor whose son is attending the group movie date is completely confident that her son and his girlfriend are really not the smooching type anyhow.

Rules for the Child's Life

I can't tell you the number of times I have dealt with this whole issue of trying to create good rules for my kids' lives. Even in our family with what I consider God's law firmly intact, there is a real struggle for good rules. Having searched the Bible high and low for helps about dating, chores, spending, TV/computer time limits, and so on, my efforts were exhaustive and frustrating—and resulted in nil as far as any help on specifics. Nothing, that is, until I was reading along in Judges of all places and found a story that helped me. There in Judges is a story about a man and his wife that outlined my parenting philosophy in regard to creating rules for my teenagers' lives.

In Judges 13, we find the man, Manoah, and his wife. His wife was barren and childless when an angel appeared to her, telling her that she would soon have a son. Completely overwhelmed with excitement, she gave the fabulous news to her husband. When Manoah heard the news, he cried out to God, begging him for instructions on how to raise the child. This is how it's recorded in Judges 13:8–12:

Then Manoah prayed to the LORD: "O Lord, I beg you, let the man of God you sent to us come again to teach us how to bring up the boy who is to be born."

God heard Manoah, and the angel of God came again to the woman while she was out in the field; but her husband Manoah was not with her. The woman hurried to tell her husband, "He's here! The man who appeared to me the other day!"

Manoah got up and followed his wife. When he came to the man, he said, "Are you the one who talked to my wife?"

"I am," he said.

So Manoah asked him, "When your words are fulfilled, what is to be the rule for the boy's life and work?"

NIV

For me, the last sentence is the enlightening part, because what it expresses are two important things every parent needs in order to create good rules for a teenager's life: faith and a yielded heart.

Let's start with the faith portion. At the time Manoah says, "When your words are fulfilled," he is giving full belief that God is faithful to his promise. He is leaning into the fact that God will enable his wife to bear a child even though she has up to now been barren. That kind of faith is just the kind of faith that delights God. Hebrews 11:6 explains it this way: "It's impossible to please God apart from faith. And why? Because anyone who wants to approach God must believe both that he exists and that he cares enough to respond to those who seek him" (Message).

In addition to faith, Manoah had a heart that was yielded to God's leadership, as evidenced by his question in Judges

13:12, "So Manoah asked him, 'When your words come true, what kind of rules should govern the boy's life and work?'" What's important to remember here is that Manoah was an Israelite—a man who loved God and understood God's laws. So he wasn't asking about whether or not the child should follow God's laws. What he was asking for was specifics from God regarding the *rules for his life.* Manoah, sensing and understanding the enormous responsibility, realized that he needed detailed operating instructions for his unborn son's life. Unbelievable foresight. Instead of adopting a wait-and-see philosophy or just testing out current parenting attitudes of the day, Manoah begged God for an appropriate parenting philosophy that he could adhere to while raising his son. He was in essence saying, "You know what's best . . . please show me your detailed plan for this kid."

In my mind, that's a great practice to live by—to have faith in what God says and to ask him to direct you specifically regarding rules for your teenager's life. Now, I know that might sound a mite simplistic and kind of pie in the sky—almost like we're expecting God to send the Ten Commandments for Teenagers down from the mountain, but let's think it through together and see if it can actually be something that can be accomplished in everyday life for you and your teenager.

Mapping Out Specific Directions

Let's say a situation comes up—like your seventeen-year-old son wants to take the car and go on a quick weekend road trip with three of his buddies to a football game. The proposed plan is to leave Saturday at noon, drive two hundred miles to another city (gargantuan in size), attend the football game (though they have no tickets yet), and then stay in a hotel close to the stadium, where they will spend the night before heading home in the morning. (Oh boy . . .)

Now, your immediate reaction might be to laugh off the suggested plan, knowing that one of the four friends is a known prankster-goofball, that getting tickets at the game is iffy, and that the destination city is known for notoriously poor navigation and aggressive drivers. And along with all that, you recall that this is the same kid who at sixteen had two fender benders within months of getting his license. In your mother heart, there is a one little word you hear over and over and over: "No. No. No!" But . . .

You are going to practice this whole idea of letting God direct the rules for your teenager's life—so, you realize you need to exhibit some faith and a yielded heart. It's having an open mind and praying something like this, "God, my first reaction to this plan is a resounding 'No!' but I realize that a lot of that is about my fears. So right now I am acknowledging that you are in control of my son's life. I want to thank you for watching over him and protecting him whether he is here at home or off somewhere else. He is your kid first and foremost, and I thank you for taking such good care of him. But I just don't think this is a good plan. It seems kind of crazy and loose ended, so I feel negatively about it. Please keep me open-minded and help me to respect my son while I am making this decision. I am also praying that you will help my son to finalize the details if it's really something that I am supposed to consider. I don't want to be overcontrolling, and I also don't want to give a blind yes without looking logically at the whole picture. Please give me your rules for his life in this situation. Amen."

This is a reaction that will get God's attention. He will answer your prayers about the rules for your teenager's life. For me, it looks a little different every time, but I promise that if you are attentive and faith filled about getting those detailed operating instructions, God will come through. It might be that your son and his friends obtain tickets to the game online instead of trying to buy them the day of the game. Or maybe instead of staying in a hotel, they agree to stay at one of the boys' relative's house twenty minutes from the stadium. The answer could come when your son sits down with you and talks about the responsibility he feels having three friends in the car when he is driving. Or maybe you know just what to do when you feel an overwhelming sense of peace about the situation, loose ended as it is, because you and your husband agree—the young man is heading out to college in a year, and he needs to figure some things out for himself.

God does not want you parenting in anxiety or ambiguity. Remember, that teenager is his, first and foremost, so he is completely thrilled that you are coming to him to find those operating instructions.

Up, Down, or on the Side

The other really important thing I have learned about designing rules for teenagers is that one set of rules does not necessarily work for every child. Now, what I am not advocating is setting up some type of indiscriminate arrangement where one of your teenagers lives by completely different standards than another; but I do advocate the necessity of altering operating instructions based on the gender, personality, and maturity of your teen.

For example, our son had certain privileges as a senior in high school that our eighteen-year-old daughter still doesn't. And the reverse is true too. When Will 3 was a senior, we allowed him more leniencies driving after midnight than we allow our daughter Emily. There were some nights when he was solo on the road at one or two in the morning. Not so with Emily. She isn't allowed to drive around late at night by herself on the streets of Austin and beyond. It's a rule we established to protect her safety. If she wants to do some running around late at night, we either encourage her to always take a friend with her or wind it up early so she's not alone after midnight. Sounds sexist, but it's not. It's a matter of realizing that women are more vulnerable and need to exercise more caution about personal safety.

Here's another example. Will's senior year, we imposed a curfew, but not with Emily during her senior year. Sounds unfair, but wait. What we found was that Emily didn't need a curfew because she wasn't much of a night owl and didn't often plan things late at night, but Will 3 was much different. He really enjoyed the freedom of running around with friends late at night, making extemporaneous plans. And while we trusted him to take good care of himself, we realized that there needed to be some kind of declarative ending point. It wasn't that we wanted Will to stop having fun; it's that we realized that a dozen high school seniors hanging out in the Wendy's parking lot videotaping each other playing simulated war games might garner unwanted attention. In reality, we were protecting Will 3 and his personal safety.

Some house rules are universal regardless of the teen. All three Davis teenagers have to make their bed in the morning (though there is a huge discrepancy on what "made" looks like), and every Davis teenager is required to sit down for a family dinner when Mom makes it. It's expected that the Davis teenagers will all attend church weekly, but there is some leniency on which of the three services they attend, allowing for autonomous decision making. And there are occasions when permission is granted to "break" a rule—like last weekend when all three of our kids requested a sleep-in Sunday. While that only happens about once or twice a year, there are some times when the "rules" are broken with parental permission.

The key to developing good rules for your teenager is to always turn to the Specialist for the best operating instructions for each teenager in your family. It's about having faith and a listening heart like Manoah. So believe and ask, because God is the one who knows best: up, down, or on the side.

PARENTING YOUR TEEN

- Think about the concept of the "law" and the "rules." What would you say are some laws for your family? What are some rules?
- How does the length of adolescence impact the need for flexibility in developing good rules for their lives?
- Is there a chance that your teenager could think that some rules are actually laws in your mind? How might

that create a kind of legalistic fear or rebellion in the life of your teenager?

- How important is it to tell your teenager that you are asking God for direction on establishing good rules for her life?
- Think of a time when you either broke one of the rules or needed to break one of the rules but didn't—how did that impact the relationship you have with your teenager?
- While it's important to pray and ask God about the rules for your child's life yourself, how might including your teenager in the prayer impact her faith? Next time a situation comes up, instead of reacting, try praying with your teen instead.

One Wise Mother

Redefining the War on Culture

This won't be your typical "the world's going to hell in a hand-basket" chapter, as I will not be ranting and raving about culture. I won't comment on the latest pop icon antics, nor will I google-fy you with horrifying stories about teenagers and MySpace. You get plenty of that every time you turn on the news. And besides that, when concerned parents watch and listen to those abased anecdotes, they tend to respond in negative ways. Like by going into hiding, literally. The plan typically involves gathering the young'uns and slamming shut the door on all things current. It's the old "if you can't beat 'em, ignore 'em" strategy. Understandable, but not entirely beneficial. The other approach is to personally engage in all-out war with modern culture and attempt to take the enemy down. The tactic is angry defiance on all things worldly. The job is to know exactly what's going on with those wretched starlets—what they're wearing, who they're kissing—and loudly put in your two cents about it, casting judgment. It's all about leading the march against this passing parade known as current culture and stomping out the heinous sinners. Understandable, but not particularly Christlike.

Instead, I want to offer you a different strategy. A strategy to get smart about you, your teenager, and the culture in which they live. I want to offer the option of becoming a wise mother where these things are concerned—a mother who has the knowledge to deal with the difficulties and dangers of modern culture, who at the same time is able to maintain a level of confidence to keep it cool under pressure. Like knowing what to do when you hear the lyrics of your daughter's favorite, albeit inappropriate, music blaring through her bedroom wall. (And it's not busting the door open and lecturing her about the musician's absolute lack of morals.) Or knowing how to handle yourself when your son brings a friend home and you stumble in the study to say hi and realize the kid is introducing your son to his favorite soft-core porn site on the Internet. (No shrieking and crying here . . . save it for later when you are telling your husband about it.) Or maybe it's something as simple as knowing what to say and do when your curvaceous fifteen-year-old attempts to walk out the door showing an eye-popping amount of cleavage. (And it's not the typical sage, starchy response, "Well, young lady, if you think you are leaving the house dressed like that, you have another thing coming!")

We live in a culture obsessed with celebrity and the latest trends. And teens are often at the center of it all. There is an entire industry focused on marketing movies, music, fashion and other products to teen audiences. So it's no wonder that many parents feel helpless trying to compete with many of the values that popular culture promotes.[1]

"Making Peace with Pop Culture," TheAntiDrug.com

The Battle Within

There are a few really important things to recognize on the road to becoming wise about culture and teens. The first is that teens have an innate desire to be familiar with and speak the language of current culture. Teenagers are inherently culture thirsty. It's as if they wake out of late childhood completely parched and dehydrated, then attempt to fuel up by pushing their face in the hydrant of popular culture. They are ready to jump in and get thoroughly doused, exposing themselves to the good and the bad. It seems one minute they were quite thrilled with Dora the Explorer and the next minute they're craving Snoop Dogg. Which leads me to the second important point, and that is that we as mothers are often overwhelmed by their yearning. Their curious thirst for all things current creates problems for us because there's a lot in culture that we don't want our kids drinking in. As a matter of fact, if we're completely honest, it's downright terrifying to think of our kids mixing it up out there. And there's a reason for that—there's a battle going on for the hearts of our teenagers. And we as mothers instinctively sense that every time they walk out the door.

It's the juxtaposition of the insatiable thirst reflected in our teenagers and the inherent dangers apparent that creates a real problem for us as mothers. But I want to propose that being afraid, overprotective, or overreactive is not the way a wise woman handles the situation. If you want to be a wise mother, you need a new battle plan. You've got to get smart in handling your culture-thirsty teenager. And I'm not talking about street smart—as in knowing all the latest teenage trends and lingo. Rather, we need the kind of smarts that come from God. I'm talking about spiritual smarts, which the Bible calls *wisdom*. Wisdom is what will keep you from being afraid of culture. Wisdom is what will keep you from being overprotective. And wisdom is what will keep you from under- or overreacting to situations. And the best thing about wisdom is that it is the only thing that will preserve your teenager's life when she is out there braving it on her own.

> Wisdom preserves the life of its possessor.
>
> Ecclesiastes 7:12 NIV

Redefining the War

If you want to help your teenager navigate culture through adolescence and beyond, you need to understand the spiritual realities of the war going on out there. Because if you happen to be crumbling under the widely accepted perception that the giant known as pop culture is an immense insurmountable enemy, then you need to know that you are smack-dab where the real enemy wants you. While there is a battle raging for the hearts and minds of our teenagers, *it is not insurmountable.* As a matter of fact, if you look at it from a spiritual perspective, *it is entirely winnable.*

Throughout history, God's people have always struggled with giants in the land, and throughout history, God has always instructed his people how to fight and win. So the truth is that we are not a unique generation facing a master-level giant. We're just a people befuddled by fear and anxiety—much like our spiritual ancestors. Let's take a look back at their experiences and learn from their situations so we can look forward with success.

Reviewing the Past to Win the Future

Enter the Israelites. Here are some people constantly overwhelmed by enormous opposition. In 1 Samuel 17, we find the Israelites in a standoff with their modern giant, Goliath. Big, hairy, and mouthy (sounds like pop culture to me), Goliath and his army of Philistines camped out, taunting the Israelite army for forty days and forty nights to engage in battle. And for forty days and forty nights, the Israelites focused on their enemy, Goliath, and were thereby paralyzed in fear.

> Then Goliath, a Philistine champion from Gath, came out of the Philistine ranks to face the forces of Israel. He was over nine feet tall! He wore a bronze helmet, and his bronze coat of mail weighed 125 pounds. He also wore bronze leg armor, and he carried a bronze javelin on his shoulder. The shaft of his spear was as heavy and thick as a weaver's beam, tipped with an iron spearhead that weighed 15 pounds. His armor bearer walked ahead of him carrying a shield. Goliath stood and shouted a taunt across to the Israelites. "Why are

you all coming out to fight?" he called. "I am the Philistine champion, but you are only the servants of Saul. Choose one man to come down here and fight me! If he kills me, then we will be your slaves. But if I kill him, you will be our slaves! I defy the armies of Israel today! Send me a man who will fight me!" When Saul and the Israelites heard this, they were terrified and deeply shaken.

vv. 4–11

I can't help but liken the reaction of the Israelites to any gathering of mothers I meet, whether it's at a basketball game or a book club. When our attention turns to the modern Goliath of pop culture, we are terrified and deeply shaken. It's as if our Goliath is shouting obscenities through all forms of media, challenging us to believe that a kid could come through adolescence as a victor. When we hear the threats of the giant, we strike a collective huddle and listen carefully. Then we focus in on how large and imposing the enemy is—by sharing horror stories about how the enemy took down one teenager or another. We sigh, overpowered and distressed, then formulate a personal plan on how we will further shield our teenager from all that's going on out there. It might be through remote surveillance monitoring of all computers in the house, or secretly checking their text messages, or maybe even sneaking a peek at a diary entry. It might be by expressly prohibiting them from ever dating. Or maybe it's keeping them away from "those" kinds of friends. The list is endless and completely unique, depending upon the parent. And while I am not trying to draw lines in the sand and specify what kinds of guidelines you as a mother need for your teenager, I do know this: When you begin to believe that the enemy is too big for your child to handle, you are likely communicating that message to your child, and the horrible thing is, they are likely to believe you. All that this negativity is doing is reinforcing the lie at hand—your teenager cannot surmount the gigantic enemy.

What I see in this generation of mothers regarding culture is this—we tend to focus on the giant instead of focusing on God. And as we gaze at Goliath, we are hypnotized by the enormous lie that the influence of pop culture is bigger than the influence of God. And we come to believe, like those frightened Israelites, that there is no way out and we're much afraid. So afraid, in fact, that we start using fear as a buffer for our false reality. Somehow we have started to believe that fearing the giant will shelter our teenagers—when in reality, we need to embrace the fact that God has ordained our kids to live in this very time period for his glory, for his purpose. And that purpose is not well served when we as mothers act as fear mongers.

The Opportunity for Victory

When we succumb to fear, we are exercising extreme forgetfulness. We are failing to remember that God is in the picture. If we can grasp the truth that God established our teenagers for this time in history, then we will realize that he uniquely equips them with the tools they need to have victory over their giants. We as mothers need to be extremely careful about holding our kids so tightly that we disable their faith. We need to make sure that our fears don't handicap their abilities. We must be willing to allow them, at the suitable age and maturity level, to engage.

This is exactly how the Israelites realized their victory in 1 Samuel 17. King Saul made a gutsy choice to allow a kid to engage in battle. After forty days and forty nights of listening to the raging of Goliath, the Israelites' unlikely little champion wandered in—and it was David, a middle school–aged sheepherder. Acting as an errand runner for his father, David wound up at the battle site, following instructions to take bread and cheese to his brothers who were fighting in the Israelite army. When he arrived and saw the soldiers run in fear from Goliath, he was appalled. So long story short, David asked permission from King Saul to fight Goliath. In 1 Samuel 17:32–37, David's appeal to the king is filled with youthful idealism:

> "Don't worry about this Philistine," David told Saul. "I'll go fight him!" "Don't be ridiculous!" Saul replied. "There's no way you can fight this Philistine and possibly win! You're only a boy, and he's been a man of war since his youth." But David persisted. "I have been taking care of my father's sheep and goats," he said. "When a lion or a bear comes to steal a lamb from the flock, I go after it with a club and rescue the lamb from its mouth. If the animal turns on me, I catch it by the jaw and club it to death. I have done this to both lions and bears, and I'll do it to this pagan Philistine, too, for he has defied the armies of the living God! The LORD who rescued me from the claws of the lion and the bear will rescue me from this Philistine!" Saul finally consented. "All right, go ahead," he said. "And may the LORD be with you!"

Now I want to insert right here that this could easily be a conversation between any worried mother and any idealistic teenager regarding our present-day Goliath of pop culture. Can't you hear it now?

Teenager: Mom, don't worry about it. I can handle it.

Mom: Don't be ridiculous! There's no way you can possibly do it! You're only a child—you have no idea what you're up against.

Teenager: Mom, I'm at that school day in and day out standing up for what I believe in. At every turn, I'm tempted to copy the culture surrounding me and compromise my values, but I don't. You have no idea how much I pray for strength and how God helps me minute by minute when I'm with friends who are encouraging me to make stupid decisions. I can do this!

Not sure a mother would be so easily convinced as King Saul. Fortunately for the Israelites, David was beseeching a king and not his mother!

From Shielding to Sieving

You see, at some point or another, we have got to believe that our kids can do this—that they can face the unique challenges shoved at them by culture and thrive. As a mother, you need to do all you can to prepare them as best you can and then let them fly. And the way we do that in a developmentally appropriate way is to stop shielding and start sieving.

For example, it is perfectly suitable to shield an elementary school child from certain television programming. In our house, that meant no MTV, VH-1, and the like. But as my kids became teenagers, I allowed a little more leeway. Like for Emily, our eighteen-year-old. She is a skilled actress, incredible dancer, and loves music—so the music videos have enormous appeal to her. And while I didn't allow her to watch those stations when she was fourteen, I do permit some of them now. Though I'm not super-wild about the programming, when it's on in the house it allows for motherly commentary. Like I might walk into the living room with a basket of laundry to fold, note what's on the screen, and say, "Wow, that sweet girl sure is exposing her ba dunk-a-dunk to the world. She must have daddy issues, poor thing." (To which Emily smirks because I almost always mispronounce when attempting to use urban street talk.) Or "Hmmm—the lyrics are so dark. What's that musician really saying? He seems so angry or something. " (To which Emily somberly nods her head yes.)

Instead of frantically screening ("Turn off that horrible, vile show!"), I'm sieving by allowing the TV to bring in the giant. And as I sieve, I speak truth over the situation without trying to sound super-preachy. I hope to expose them to some critical thinking about the war going on. And by just being there, I offer a presence—hopefully a godly one—that communicates calm, cool, and wise. Very wise.

Now, lest you misunderstand what I am saying, let me clarify. I am *not* advocating a carte blanche approach by letting them watch or do whatever they want and then trying to sprinkle in a little Scripture. For example, I have no plans of having a big beer bash followed by a Bible study at my house. Nor would I passively sit by, allowing any of my teenagers to view pornography under my care, "sieving" as they go. That's stupid.

But I will say this—if I did stumble upon one of them viewing something inappropriate on the computer, I would sit down right next to them, click the images away, and with tears running down my cheeks, I take advantage of the opportunity to speak truth about the giant right there while they are under my care. I would talk bluntly about what they were viewing, how it derogates women and humans in general, and how it breaks God's heart. I would thoroughly explain that pornography wrecks the beauty of a healthy sexual relationship in marriage. I hope I wouldn't shame them, but rather would speak the truth forcefully and in love. And then I would ask them to pray with me that God would strengthen them not to enter into the stranglehold of the enemy.

I have chosen sieving over shielding as my kids get older because I understand how things work with teenagers: they leave. As unexpected as it will seem when your first teenager leaves the house, they all go. Each one will set off to college or a job, and when they go, they will be completely exposed to the giant. I have come to realize that if I have shielded and never sieved, I am placing them in a weakened state before the enemy. Either a state of complete naiveté about what to think in regard to culture or a state of utter fear and failing about handling the battle alone.

Steps to Becoming a Battle-Wise Mom

We know how important it is for any military force to be armed and ready when entering a battle—so how do we arm and ready ourselves for the daily battles we face? The best first step to becoming battle wise is to get fresh wisdom from the source. That would be the Word. While it's great to read books about teens and culture or attend seminars, the number one thing you can do is read the Bible. I highly recommend reading the Bible cover to cover, but for the purposes of this chapter, I will highlight some specific books I feel touch on the matter at hand.

For understanding everyday wisdom, I would say read Ecclesiastes. It's a book written by Solomon (King David's son) and is actually nicknamed the "book of wisdom." This book will help you take a deep breath and realize that "there is nothing new under the sun" where God is concerned. Ecclesiastes is a refreshing sip of water when I feel the bottom is falling out in this parched land we live in. Read and be comforted.

Another book that is entirely applicable is Proverbs. It's packed with handy sayings for real life. These verses are especially helpful to me when making motherly commentary, though I often paraphrase them. One of my all-time favorites is Proverbs 27:12, which I use when one of my girls is going to be out and about at night. The Susie Davis paraphrase is, "It's scaryville out there. Stay aware. Gotta be smart and think ahead." Check out the real version and see how you might paraphrase for your teenagers in various situations.

Another book that helps me, especially emotionally, is the book of Psalms. I can't tell you how many times I have felt God directly comfort me regarding one of my teenagers. You will find your heart in the Psalms. My latest prayer and confession for my kids is Psalm 89:17, "You are their glorious strength. Our power is based on your favor."

Finally, read the Gospel accounts: Matthew, Mark, Luke, and John. In reading these accounts of the life of Jesus, you will gain knowledge and wisdom in knowing how to be a more Jesus-y mother. The most profound revelation I received about Jesus and culture while reading the Gospels is this: He didn't try to change culture. He never marched in a parade against anything, no matter how vile. The only thing he defined as vile was religious hypocrisy. He went after the sanctimonious hypocrites. But he never set cultural change as his goal. Instead, he demonstrated how to be godly in culture. Check out the Sermon on the Mount.

The second important step to take is to ask God for help. Be ready to ask God directly for wisdom about how to handle your teenager. Pray, pray. pray. Ask, ask, ask.

King Solomon had the right idea—no doubt he was following in his daddy's footsteps. When he was appointed king over the nation of Israel, he realized he needed help, and so he asked. In 2 Chronicles 1:7–10, we find the encounter between God and Solomon. "That night God appeared to Solomon. God said, 'What do you want from me? Ask.' Solomon answered, 'You were extravagantly generous with David my father, and now you have made me king in his place. Establish, GOD, the words you spoke to my father, for you've given me a staggering task, ruling this mob of people. Yes, give me wisdom and knowledge as I come and go among this people—for who on his own is capable of leading these, your glorious people?'" (Message).

That's actually an appropriate ask for a mother of teenagers, don't you think? We have a staggering task here and a small mob of people we're entrusted to manage. We desperately need wisdom and knowledge to lead "these, your glorious people." We need to stop feeling beaten down and go to the source of all wisdom and ask. Let's get about the business of asking God at every turn how to lead these glorious teenagers he has given us.

> If any of you lacks wisdom, he should ask God, who gives generously to all without finding fault, and it will be given to him.
>
> James 1:5 NIV

Finally, you need to remember an all-important truth as confessed by David right before he killed Goliath in 1 Samuel 17:45–47. Here's what this middle school–aged boy had to say upon commencing with the battle against his giant:

> David answered, "You come at me with sword and spear and battle-ax. I come at you in the name of GOD-of-the-Angel-Armies, the God of Israel's troops, whom you curse and mock. This very day GOD is handing you over to me. I'm about to kill you, cut off your head, and serve up your body and the bodies of your Philistine buddies to the crows and coyotes. The whole earth will know that there's an extraordinary God in Israel. And everyone gathered here will learn that GOD doesn't save by means of sword or spear. The battle belongs to GOD—he's handing you to us on a platter!"
>
> Message

Battle-wise moms! We serve an extraordinary God, and the battle belongs to him!

■ ■ ■ ■ ■ ■ ■ ■ ■

PARENTING YOUR TEEN

- What are some of the biggest cultural giants your teenager is facing? Or the biggest giants facing teenagers at large?
- How does your internal battle regarding culture influence your parenting?
- What are you most afraid of when thinking of your teenager and the influence of pop culture? How does that influence your parenting decisions?

- How is your teenager's opportunity for victory dependent upon you?
- What are some practical ways to move from shielding to sieving?
- What are three things you can do to get braver on behalf of your teenager?

7

Exorcising Emotionalism

Tips for Regaining Control

I'd really like to write a book on self-control, but then you might erroneously think that I'm super-skinny and that I've never bounced a check. Or you might assume that I have a tranquil, calm life replete with an überorganized, color-coded calendar. That's probably what I would surmise about an author writing a book on living a self-controlled life. I would naturally believe that the author has it *all together*. And though I would be interested, of course, in getting it all together, I would be very wary of a published piece by some hoity-toity writer that made me feel like a complete loser because I wasn't just like her.

Well, let me reassure you: I must constantly watch my weight, my bank balance, and my busy calendar. I wake every day with a mental list of things I'd like to improve about myself. I am a Christian and I believe that God is in the process of making me better, but I also still struggle daily with sin and shortcoming. I am a regular woman in need of some self-control—over my habits, my impulses, and my appetites.

But there is another important reason I need self-control, and it's a reason not many people think about—*self-control preserves relationships*. Consider that for just a minute. Now maybe you're racking your brain and thinking, "Well, okay . . . yes, I kinda get that. Getting control over my eating habits would probably help me be a better mother because I would be so much happier if I lost twenty pounds and that in turn would make me easier to be around. And yes, I can see how getting rid of the unnecessary debt would definitely lessen the stress in the house. And certainly, if my schedule was more organized, I would be much more efficient. Like a CEO—all cool, calm, and collected. Hmmm, yes, I am starting to see how all that would make me a happier, healthier mom and then I'd have a better relationship with my kids."

That's all well and good, but more importantly, self-control is a valuable trait to keep from overindulging feelings and saying and doing things that you otherwise had no intention of saying and doing. Remember back to the last time you got really angry and lost it with your teenager. Or think about a time when you got terribly emotional—really over the top. Maybe your teenager said something incredibly hurtful, like "I hate you!" or "You're such a hypocrite!" Or maybe they did something stupid, like wreck the car for the second time in a month. Now be honest here—what did you say and what did you do? In the heat of the moment did you let your true feelings fly? Did your frustrations mount to the point that they overwhelmed reason? Did you say or do things you shouldn't have and wind up hurting your teenager?

When things happen that are unexpected and upsetting, emotions swell. And there's nothing wrong with that. But if your feelings swell to the point that they overwhelm your capacity to be mature and motherly, then you've got a problem. Self-control is the thing that will help you manage the feelings that inevitably surface.

Mature and Motherly?

I know "mature and motherly" sounds downright matronly—not how any of us want to be characterized. As a matter of fact, I get a visual of a woman with graying, fuzzy hair whipped into an upright bun, tortoise-shell reading glasses perched on the end of her nose, and a plump, unkempt body draped in a pale peach muumuu. But that's not the maturity I'm getting at here. I am talking about inner maturity, the kind of inside attitude that produces adult responses to those erratic situations that come up in your life.

I can think of tons of examples when I have not behaved in a mature and motherly fashion. Just tons. But the one that keeps surging to the surface centers around a time when we were in Colorado on a family vacation.

> The wise woman builds her house, but with her own hands the foolish one tears hers down.
>
> Proverbs 14:1

Now, what you must know before I start this story is that I married into a family of hikers and climbers. As a matter of fact, my husband's family has a cabin in Estes Park, Colorado, smack-dab in the middle of Rocky Mountain National Park. So when I married into the family, it was kind of a given that I would hike. But what I discovered as a newbie Davis in those early years of marriage is that the true test of any "real" Davis was to hike the big one: Longs Peak. Longs Peak stands at 14,259 feet above sea level. It's a monstrous mountain. Reaching the summit requires a sixteen-mile trek that typically takes about twelve hours to complete. The hike must be started at one o'clock in the morning to avoid dangerous weather, and if you're lucky and the weather doesn't stop you, you just might get to the top alive. Okay, I may be exaggerating a little bit, but it is true that at least one hiker dies on Longs every year.

I knew about the risks when I agreed to hike Longs with my husband the summer of 2000. I also understood that *some people* considered it treacherous—though none of those people were my in-laws. So after fifteen years of marriage, I psyched myself up and decided to become a "real" Davis.

The first couple hours of the hike were relatively easy. Just a lot of walking in the dark through Goblin Forest (not joking on the name here), teeny tiny flashlight in hand, wondering if bears were tracking us. Then as the sun broke over the horizon, we spent another couple hours hiking the Boulder Field—not bad, except for the serious effort required to suck in massive amounts of air, which is a necessity at 12,000 feet. But when we got to the Keyhole (an amazing sight to see) and actually stepped through to the back side of Longs, the real fun started.

You know, the kind of fun you have when you realize that if you slip or misstep, you will die! That kind of fun.

There was no proper trail at all, only yellow and red bull's-eyes spray painted by the nice park rangers every so often on the sheer ledge ahead. The bull's-eyes were there to show you where you were supposed to body-hug the mountain. That's the fun I knew firsthand as I stood facing the particular part of Longs known as The Ledges . . . the very place where I realized I didn't care about being a "real" Davis anymore and even contemplated whether I wanted to be a Davis at all! Needless to say, it was a hard hike on my nerves and our marriage. What I theorized there on The Ledges as I body-hugged that mountain and inched my way angrily to the summit was that if I slipped and started to fall, Will would reach out to try and save me. Then we would both tumble tragically to our deaths, and our three young children would be orphans.

Thankfully, my worst fears were never realized, and although I can't say I enjoyed the experience, I got down alive with my marriage intact (barely). However, when I got back to the cabin some seventeen hours later, I made a little secret promise to myself: none of my children would ever become "real" Davises.

So the very next year when we made our annual trek to Estes Park and my thirteen-year-old son approached me while we were at the Fourth of July fireworks show and said, "Mom, Dad and I really want to hike Longs tomorrow," I completely freaked. I started crying, slowly at first, with just a few little tears leaking out. But as my son kept talking (and my husband kept agreeing with him), I got more and more emotional. I felt complete distress over his proposal—and I felt incredibly angry with my husband for even considering it. I remember leaning against our Suburban, letting myself sink down, down, down into what I was feeling. The fear, the worry, the anger. And as I looked out at the black night, fireworks blasting across the sky, I remember feeling like that was exactly what was going on in my heart. Emotions exploding unexpectedly, sparks flying everywhere, enticing me to surrender to the chaos I was feeling.

Because of my emotional fit, the guys canceled their man plan. I was quite happy about that decision. My feelings were soothed and quiet. Instead of Longs, they hiked the comparatively docile Chapin, Chiquita, and Ypsilon Mountains—better known as CC&Y.

The Spirit Is Willing, But the Flesh Is Weak

What I realize now is that the overemotionalism I struggled with at the fireworks display was very much like what I faced that morning on The Ledges at Longs Peak—they were both emotional battles. And by all accounts, you could say that I won one and I lost one.

Let me explain. When I was on The Ledges, I fought with everything I had to make it to the top. I even remember throwing off my backpack and leaving it on the mountain so I could maneuver carefully to the top. I put *everything I had into a successful and safe summit*. But when it came time to summit my circumstances that evening of the Fourth, I folded. I succumbed to my feelings, allowing them to take priority over my capacity to be reasonable. Overriding my capacity to be "mature and motherly."

Now lest you misunderstand, what I failed to mention in recalling my hiking experience is that there were teenagers going up Longs that year my husband and I went. (Not my teenagers, of course.) And the truth is, my nephews and nieces hiked Longs with their parents at twelve and thirteen years old. See, the thing is that it was an emotional, scary situation for me and I didn't like it, but it wasn't necessarily a dangerous situation overall. Did climbing that mountain require focused energy? Sure. Careful concentration? You bet. Was I overreacting to the situation? Well, maybe . . .

But there was a reason I reacted emotionally when Will 3 asked to hike Longs. *I felt like it.* My feelings said, "Cry, cry, cry. Now cry harder. Be pitiful. Moan. You can keep them from their lunacy. Cry until they see things your way." And so I did. And I got my way. But the problem is that I was listening to the wrong thing. I was yielding to the flesh—not the spirit. In Romans 7:18–19, Paul describes the schizophrenic distress when caught between operating in the spirit and in the flesh. He says, "And I know that nothing good lives in me, that is, in my sinful nature. I want to do what is right, but I can't. I want to do what is good, but I don't. I don't want to do what is wrong, but I do it anyway." That is the nature of the flesh, or the sin nature. The flesh is the thing that prompts immature behavior—like becoming overly emotional to get your way. It is the very thing in us that indulges our selfish side. It's what makes grown-ups act very childish. Conversely, the spirit is the part that's mature. It is levelheaded and thinks of others first. It is considerate and thoughtful, even when pressed.

The problem comes in when there is a test and I am unprepared—like the surprise at the fireworks display. Uncontrolled feelings instantly swell to the surface, intending to overtake me, and then I get a prompt from my spiritual side to disengage those maverick emotions. And suddenly, I have a war going on in the inner man. Or should I say, the inner woman.

That evening of the Fourth, I didn't put up a fight to do the right thing and behave reasonably. I pretty much gave in to the emotional, selfish side. How do I know that? Because after crying and carrying on, then getting the guys to go with my plan, I felt a teeny, tiny spark of remorse. And then after the dust settled, I felt embarrassed about my "breakdown." And I realized in that situation, I was just like Paul—I wanted to do what was good, but I didn't. I didn't want to do what was wrong, but I did it anyway. Poop.

Of course, the thing about living in the flesh is that you get the reward of the flesh. And in my case, I credit my fit with sending my guys up a different mountain that next morning. A much "safer" one. Remember docile CC&Y? Well, it ended up being the most disastrous thing that has happened to our family while hiking in Colorado. In a nutshell, while my husband was helping a friend, Will 3 took a turn that landed him on the wrong side of the mountain by himself for over two hours. The park ranger was called in, my poor husband was completely frantic, and my son was having a horrific hiking experience. A thirteen-year-old kid lost in the Rockies by himself is a bad scene.

The Fruit of Self-Control

So how can we live above our feelings? What does it look like to live a life that's not driven by the flesh? And how do we specifically deal with the feelings that anger, hurt, or fear bring forth without doing the wrong thing? We live by yielding to God's Holy Spirit in our life. We pray and ask for help when we are on the hike of our life, struggling toward the summit. What's really amazing (and encouraging) is that the Bible tells us that if we are believers, we have self-control. It's tucked deep inside our spirit, ready to engage at a moment's notice. Galatians 5:22–23 says, "But the Holy Spirit produces this kind of fruit in our lives: love, joy, peace, patience, kindness, goodness, faithfulness, gentleness, and self-control. There is no law against these things!"

So okay, you might be thinking, if I am a Christian and the Bible says I already have self-control, why don't I see the "fruit" of it in my life? A reasonable question and one I have thought on for some time. I don't think there's a quick-fix answer, but I do think there are several things at play when it comes to exercising self-control in our relationships.

The first is that growing things takes time. If self-control is likened to fruit, isn't it reasonable that it has to germinate? It's not like you pray to become a Christian and your whole personality changes. No. You pray, and then slowly and surely you grow spiritually. And as you grow, you change. But I

I've tried everything and nothing helps. I'm at the end of my rope. Is there no one who can do anything for me? Isn't that the real question? The answer, thank God, is that Jesus Christ can and does. He acted to set things right in this life of contradictions where I want to serve God with all my heart and mind, but am pulled by the influence of sin to do something totally different.

Romans 7:24–25 Message

also believe that it's essential to recognize the need for help and to ask for it. Because it's only in asking God for help that you develop the self-control seed that is already present there. His presence in your life makes that kind of maturity evident. And you further develop that virtue when you read the Bible, pray, and yield to the Holy Spirit's promptings. That's when you grow.

The second thing is that you have to protect the fruit in your life and nurture it. We have this fabulous apple tree in our backyard, and every year it produces tons of apples. But just as surely as those apples show up, the squirrels shimmy up that tree, snag the apples, take one bite, and toss them to the ground, thereby ruining the fruit. They're such a nuisance. Just the other day, my daughter Sara witnessed one of the rodents doing damage, and she said, "Mom, those squirrels are eating all the apples off our tree again. Can't we wrap the trunk in something to keep them from taking all the fruit?" And I thought, yes, apparently we need a plan to keep those nasty varmints off the tree. While it would be great to live in a squirrel-free neighborhood, it's not likely to happen any time soon, so if I really want that fruit, I must get a proactive plan.

Well, the same is true with the fruit of self-control in your life. While it would be fabulous if your family situation was squirrel free—with no one darting around intentionally or unintentionally pushing your emotional buttons—it's not realistic. So it becomes necessary to do things that protect the fruit of self-control in your life. I happen to think the best way to protect self-control is to exercise it and strengthen it. I look for opportunities to cultivate self-control, practicing it, so that it becomes more of a normal reaction for me— like a habit.

Cultivating Self-Control

The deal with cultivating self-control emotionally is that it requires the same practice as developing self-control physically. If you want to lose ten pounds, you create a daily diet plan that limits how much you will eat. And that diet is only successful if you stick with your plan, come what may. Whether you are at home eating alone or out eating with friends. Whether you're at a fast-food restaurant or at your favorite sit-down spot. Good food, bad food, no matter what the circumstances, your diet will only be successful if *you* stick to the plan. It's nobody else's job and it's nobody else's fault if you do or don't stick to it—it's up to you and you alone.

The same is true when you exercise self-control in your relationships. You will only succeed by sticking with God's plan, come what may. Since the Bible tells us to "be agreeable, be sympathetic, be loving, be compassionate, be humble. That goes for all of you, no exceptions. No retaliation. No sharp-tongued sarcasm. Instead, bless—that's your job, to bless. You'll be a blessing and also get a blessing" (Message), as it says in 1 Peter 3:8–9, then we must commit to that kind of relational "diet." And the same applies when you read James 1:19–21 and find it instructs you to "lead with your ears, follow up with your tongue, and let anger straggle along in the rear. God's righteousness doesn't grow from human anger. So throw all spoiled virtue and cancerous evil in the garbage. In simple humility, let our gardener, God, landscape you with the Word, making a salvation-garden of your life" (Message).

God's Word provides the diet for cultivating self-control in relationships. When you have self-control because you are sticking to God's plan, then it doesn't matter what others are saying or doing. And it won't even matter how you are *feeling*. No matter how mad you feel, there will be no "retaliation" or no "sharp-tongued sarcasm"; instead, you will "lead with your ears, follow with your tongue and let anger straggle along in the rear." It's only then that you will have peaceable relationships, because you are choosing to exorcize the emotionalism to regain control. This is something that you can learn, and it will take time, but with God's help it can be done. And when it's been accomplished, there's really no better feeling in the world.

I should know . . . because my husband and son finally did get to take that hike up Longs Peak. And I am genuinely happy to say, that it was one of the best experiences they've ever shared!

■ ■ ■ ■ ■ ■ ■ ■ ■

Parenting your teen

- The capacity for being self-controlled physically does not always equate with being self-controlled emotionally? Why not? Are there some skills that translate from the physical arena to the emotional arena and vice versa?
- Think of the ways your teenagers push your buttons. Is there a consistent theme that could explain what bothers you most?
- While the Bible exhorts us to exercise self-control, it doesn't mandate that we control others. How might some of the button pushing be connected to you trying to control your teenager?

- The Bible mentions various ways to handle anger. In Ephesians 4:25–27 it says, "Therefore each of you must put off falsehood and speak truthfully to his neighbor, for we are all members of one body. 'In your anger do not sin': Do not let the sun go down while you are still angry, and do not give the devil a foothold" (NIV). And in Psalm 4:4 it says, "In your anger do not sin; when you are on your beds, search your hearts and be silent" (NIV). How are both passages legitimately Spirit-led ways to handle anger when you are stirred up emotionally?

- James 1:26 is a hard-core verse about controlling the tongue. It says, "If you claim to be religious but don't control your tongue, you are fooling yourself, and your religion is worthless." Why is it that our words play such a strong role in indicting our faith?

- What steps can you take to cultivate emotional self-control? How might a stricter scriptural "diet" impact your relationships at home?

Overbooked

Helping Your Teen Manage School Stress

I would guess it's no surprise to you that teenagers are feeling entirely stressed out about their lives. They are often overworked, overscheduled, and suffering as a result of it. As a matter of fact, it's not at all unusual to hear about teenagers with the same types of stress-related maladies as many adults. But what you might find surprising is exactly what teens are stressed out about. Although you might think that most teenagers are concerned about how well they perform on the basketball team and how good they look when they walk out the door, that's not what's stressing them out. In a recent survey conducted by MTV (of all things) and the Associated Press, the most often cited stressor among thirteen-to-seventeen-year-olds is school.[1] That's interesting, don't you think? Not the kind of thing you and I were consumed with as teenagers, but times have changed. Over the last few decades, dramatic academic reforms have increased the pressure on kids of all ages to perform at a rigorous standard scholastically—and for many, the pressure starts as early as kindergarten. In a *Newsweek* article, "Too Much Too Soon," writer Peg Tyre uncovers where the seed is sown.

> In the last decade, the earliest years of schooling have become less like a trip to "Mister Rogers Neighborhood" and more like SAT prep. Thirty years ago first grade was for learning how to read. Now, reading lessons start in kindergarten and kids who don't crack the code by the middle of first grade get extra help. Instead of story time, finger painting, tracing letters, and snack, first graders are spending hours doing math sheets and sounding out words in reading groups. In some places recess, music, art and even social studies are being replaced by writing exercises and spelling quizzes. Kids as young as 6 are tested, and tested again—some every 10 days or so—to ensure they're making progress. After school, there's homework, and for some, educational videos, more workbooks and tutoring to help give them an edge.[2]

The educational edge. It starts in kindergarten and lasts all the way through high school, where we find many teenagers in the ultimate quest for the perfect academic résumé. There's nothing wrong with that. But if getting that edge culminates in stress and anxiety at any point, it can be extremely unhealthy, and from all appearances, that's the formula culture is charting for our children. In a report for the American Academy of Pediatrics, adolescent-medicine specialist Kenneth Ginsburg concluded that stress for teens is definitely on the rise, leaving some kids grappling with overwhelming anxiety and even depression.[3] Interestingly enough, Ginsburg linked much of the ongoing stress to one source: college acceptance. With universities expecting more and more in the way of packed résumés, teenagers nationwide are feeling the crunch of being all things to all people to get into their college of choice. And this anxiety isn't just for the students. The truth is that the pressure is mounting and their parents are feeling the pinch too.

Marilee Jones, the dean of admissions at Massachusetts Institute of Technology and the mother of a teenager, knows the pressure firsthand. She sees well-qualified students being turned away from MIT every year, so when her daughter entered seventh grade, she sat her down to have an honest talk: "I remember [telling] her she has to get ready for high school, she needs to develop activities, she needs to have interests, she needs to develop passions. And I remember that she looked at me like she had no idea what I was talking about."[4] A few months following the "passions" pep talk, her daughter began having stomach pain. They made a visit to the doctor to find out that the likely culprit was stress. Jones confessed, "There was nothing wrong with her. It was all coming from me."[5]

Her confession was interesting and made me wonder if maybe it's not just the teacher or the school that cause my teenager to stress over class work. Perhaps there's something else here at play, and maybe it has to do with an unfairly elevated or impractical educational expectation I have for my teenager—or even one that she has for herself. Though it would be great to be able to point the finger at schools like MIT for having unreachable standards, the greater truth could be that achieving the mandatory "edge" necessary to be accepted by such institutions is illusionary and unrealistic for *my* child.

On the Edge of Anxiety

This whole notion of feeling pressured by unrealistic expectations is not new. But the fact that unwitting parents like you and me could be pushing our own children to achieve scholastic success at the risk of their emotional well-being is unthinkable. It happens innocently enough. You attend the Back to School night at the middle school and hear all about what it has to offer. They describe the college prep track, where the middle school pre-AP (Advanced Preparation) classes lead to high school AP classes, which in turn lead to a fabulous acceptance letter from a major university, and you think, "But of course! Sign my son up. There's nothing he can't do—there's no place he

The drive to succeed should be in balance with a child's capabilities. We see some adolescents who are burning out. In the middle of their sophomore, junior or senior year, their interest in school dissipates, their focus and concentration and drive start to fade. We see average students who are pressured to achieve above and beyond what they're capable of, or where their best interest lies. And we see an impact on self-esteem and confidence, as well as things like anxiety and depression, starting to emerge in these children.[6]

Child psychologist Michelle Kees

can't go!" You're aiming high for your child—as you should. It's wonderful to have a mother believe in the potential of her child. But be very careful . . . because aiming high without being willing to constantly flex and adapt your expectations based on the realities of your child's strengths, weaknesses, and willingness can cause undue pressure on the relationship.

For example, let's say you have a terrifically motivated seventh-grade son. He loves school, is naturally gifted, and does exceedingly well without any external motivation from his teacher or Mom and Dad. But then as the years roll by, something happens. The hormones kick in, and you can see that his brain is clearly undergoing a remodel, as evidenced by his behavior. And then slowly but surely your once stellar student is bringing home grades that are lackluster to say the least.

So you talk with your son. You reason with your son. You tell him he is far more capable than his 74.3 average. And maybe he even agrees with you, but apparently it does nothing to motivate his effort. So you let a few weeks go by and you have *another* talk, but still no improvement, so you try grounding him from things that seem to matter, like his cell phone . . . then the television . . . and finally the car. Still nothing. And this cycle continues until the report card finally comes home and you see that he is barely skimming by with a C average in three classes. You're at your wit's end with him. It seems that he is dropkicking his current opportunities and his future success. You feel that his GPA is trashed, his résumé wrecked, and the most important bridges are burning—the ones that will enable him to go to the college of his choice.

It saddens you and angers you and frustrates you all at the same time. Then the tension mounts between the two of you when your expectations and the reality of his academic performance slam into each other at full force. There's a rift in the relationship. And you think, if only his grades would improve, things would be better between you. But honestly, allowing performance to set the watermark for the relationship is not only dangerous, it's ungodly. And the trouble is, there will always be things about your kid's résumé that will frustrate you. What you really need is to be willing to look at this from another angle. Doing so will safeguard the relationship—and secure the best success for your teenager.

The Twenty-Year Perspective

You might need what my friend Rick calls "the twenty-year perspective." It goes something like this: Twenty years from now, what will matter most . . . your son's high school résumé or your relationship with him (and his wife and your grandchildren)? Twenty years from now, what will be most important . . . a graduate degree or the legacy of healthy family relationships? Twenty years from now, will you care most about the man he's become or the job that he holds? Twenty years from now, will you feel grateful you pushed your teenager relentlessly to achieve high marks, or will you feel glad that you refused to obsess about the C- and enjoyed the time with your teenager instead?

The great thing about imagining things twenty years from now is that it will help you to realize that some of the hyper-attention you are giving your teenager's high school report

Kids aren't having the experiences that are mandatory for healthy child development—and that's a period of time to be left alone, to figure out who you are, to experiment with different things, to fail, and to develop a repertoire of responses to challenge. They have no interior life. It's all about performance—and performance is not real learning.[7]

Psychologist and author Madeline Levine

card is just plain misplaced passion. While you want the best for your teenager, if the best doesn't fit the precise calculation culture requires, then you have to admit—that's not what you want. Recognizing this truth will help you understand that while your intentions might be good, they might not be wise. Especially if that hyperattention is wrecking your relationship. As mothers, we need to exercise enormous amounts of wisdom regarding our expectations. We need to be committed to a parenting curriculum of perspective and grace and wisdom. We need to realize that not every child will thrive in every subject at every level, but that doesn't mean that they won't be a success in life.

I wish you could have been with me in Washington DC last May. My husband Will and I made all the great stops: the Lincoln Memorial, the Capitol, the White House. But my most memorable visit was to the National Archives Building. There was an exhibit there called "School House to White House: The Education of the Presidents." The exhibit housed nostalgic pieces from the educational experiences of every American president since Herbert Hoover, with more than one hundred and fifty documents and mementos.

There was some incredibly interesting stuff, like twelve-year-old Richard Milhous Nixon's essay on how he "would like to study law and enter politics for an occupation so that I might be of some good to the people."[8] But the documents that really captured my attention were the report cards revealing the good, the bad, and the ugly. There were dozens of eye-popping reports, but one in particular was especially startling. It was a report card from December of 1930 for a thirteen-year-old boy attending Canterbury School (college prep and boarding school in New Milford, Connecticut). The card was marked as follows: 71.69 in English, 64.35 in Latin, 67 in History (his favorite subject), 61.69 in Math, 66.62 in Science, and a 78.46 in Religion. Can you guess which US president owned that stellar 77 overall average at thirteen? John Fitzgerald Kennedy.

Upon further investigation, I found his high school records weren't much better. As a matter of fact, his grades were so poor at Choate boarding school that his dad sent him a little motivational letter addressing the problem. An excerpt from the letter follows:

> Now Jack, I don't want to give the impression that I am a nagger, for goodness knows I think that is the worst thing any parent can be, and I also feel that you know if I didn't really feel you had the goods I would be most charitable in my attitude toward your failings. After long experience in sizing up people I definitely know you have the goods and you can go a long way . . .
>
> It is very difficult to make up fundamentals that you have neglected when you were very young, and that is why I am urging you to do the best you can. I am not expecting too much, and I will not be disappointed if you don't turn out to

be a real genius, but I think you can be a really worthwhile citizen with good judgment and understanding.[9]

I love that letter. It represents a father who had the wisdom to realize that "being a nagger is the worst thing any parent can be," but at the same time he understood the necessity to encourage responsibility. And while reading his letter, I started to wonder if maybe he was exercising the twenty-year perspective for his son when he said, "I think you can be a really worthwhile citizen with good judgment and understanding."

Don't Let Schooling Interfere with Your Education

My father-in-law is a man indebted to education. He was raised in a single-parent home by a schoolteacher mother who scrimped and scraped to get by. And though she never made much money, she did raise a man who not only completed college and law school but also went on to serve on multiple educational boards, including serving as the chairman of the Board of Regents at Baylor University. One of the reasons I love my father-in-law is because he exhibits pragmatism and wisdom regarding schooling and children. As a matter of fact, one of his favorite quips is Mark Twain's legendary quote, "Don't let schooling interfere with your education." My father-in-law has used this quote on more occasions than I can remember and always in an attempt to calm and cool otherwise anxious children and grandchildren stressing over school. What my father-in-law knows is this: a good "education" extends far beyond the hours spent poring over books in school. And he encourages us to be the kind of people that know the difference—and live accordingly.

I have to admit, I feel I have a ways to go to get to that level of mastery in real life. But I have learned a few lessons that bear repeating.

The first is to *live and love in the present*. When we, as mothers, obsess over preparing our teens for the future, we lose the ability to enjoy them *today*. When you are worried and anxious for your kids, it's hard to remember to appreciate them—just the way they are. Ask any mother of grown children if she regrets time spent worrying and nagging her kids through high school, or if she regrets not expressing acceptance for those kids through high school, accepting them come what may. Does she wish she had spent more time verbalizing disappointment or giving encouragement? More time pouting or praising? We need to constantly remember

From my perspective at MIT, I have deep fears about the future of innovation. I don't see as much individual creativity anymore among applicants. They're so busy, they don't have a chance to daydream. They're just moving from activity to activity to activity to try to satisfy the needs of all the adults in their lives. The Thomas Edisons of the nation, the individuals who will change the world, I don't see that. And that has dire consequences for our nation's ability to compete. . . . In this country's system of education, there is this kind of weird drive to try to mold kids a certain way and not really value who they are.[10]

Marilee Jones, admissions dean,
Massachusetts Institute of Technology

that our teenagers aren't projects—they're people. They are people who need grace and mercy—and sometimes a kick in the butt—but mainly, love. They are people just like you and me. It's that kind of understanding that will help remind us to prize the relationship with them over any performance scholastical or otherwise. And it's then that we will love them the way Jesus loves us.

The second is to *place a premium on spiritual success over scholastic success.* I won't soon forget my husband's wise words spoken as I fumed and fretted over the C one of my teenagers brought home. He said, "Susie, I would much rather have a teenager making a C in chemistry who knows how to choose between right and wrong than have a Rhodes Scholar with no moral compass at all." Enough said—perspective gained. I changed my goals from worrying about scholastic achievement to being grateful for spiritual maturity.

Finally, be sure to *acknowledge the experts.* I have to confess that I've had some experts help me along the way. They are the people I must recognize as the real professionals, for they are the ones who didn't shut me out when I was overbearing. They loved me when I blundered through, whether I was attempting to hypermanage homework sessions or obsessing about a GPA. They're my teenagers. And they are the ones I credit with teaching me a thing or two about life and grace and education. Author Anna Quindlen credits her team of experts just beautifully:

> Even today I'm not sure what worked and what didn't, what was me and what was simply life. When they were very small, I suppose I thought someday they would become who they were because of what I'd done. Now I suspect

> Nothing could make me happier than getting reports that my children continue diligently in the way of Truth!
>
> 3 John 4 Message

they simply grew into their true selves because they demanded in a thousand ways that I back off and let them be. The books said to be relaxed and I was often tense, matter-of-fact and I was sometimes over the top. And look how it all turned out. I wound up with the three people I like best in the world, who have done more than anyone to excavate my essential humanity. That's what the books never told me. I was bound and determined to learn from the experts. It just took me a while to figure out who the experts were.[11]

PARENTING YOUR TEEN

- Take an honest look at your teenager's life. Specifically, what kind of school stress does your teen experience most? Psychologists tell us that there is bad stress that tears down and good stress that motivates. Would you say that your teen is getting torn down or motivated by the current school responsibilities?

- Most teens these days have loads of extracurricular activities. Ecclesiastes 3:1 says, "There is a time for everything, and a season for every activity under heaven" (NIV). Is there a chance that some of those activities have exceeded their expiration date? What steps can you take to help your teenager wisely manage extracurricular activities?

- Many teenagers struggle in managing their time. How can you help your teen determine if it's the subject matter or inadequate time management?

- At what point does a teenager deserve the right to have ownership over their study habits regardless of how stupid they might seem?

- Are there school-related issues you could overlook to maintain the health of your relationship with your teenager? What are they?

- Ultimately, the best thing your teenager could attain to is pleasing God. What conversations could you have with your teen to encourage accountability to God for their schoolwork? Is there a chance God is happy with their effort but you are not?

- Parents seem to fall into two categories with their teenagers where school stress is concerned. Either they have unrealistic expectations or they suffer from an inability to model a sane family schedule. Which of the following mock-up class descriptions best suits your needs as a mom?

    Statistics—This course focuses on the fact that statistically there are no perfect high school résumés. The basis of the class will be to remind mothers of the improbability of consistently perfect scores on her teenager's report cards. Case studies will include reviewing historical documents including but not limited to report cards from the mother's academic résumé as well as interviews from former teachers as required.

    Recreation Studies (required lab)—This course focuses on the idea of recreation as a form of therapy. Content includes ideas and procedures for promoting a restful schedule. Hands-on leisure experience is required, as well as time spent allowing teens to complain of boredom. **Note:** (1) Laboratory requires dissection of teen's schedule. Individual after-school activities will be dissected, evaluated, and eliminated as necessary. The course prerequisite must include prayer and rest from current schedule as determined by Advisor.

Additional Recommended Resources

Cheri Fuller, *Unlocking Your Child's Learning Potential: How to Equip Kids to Succeed in School & Life* (Colorado Springs: Pinon Press, 1994).

Kathy Koch, *How Am I Smart? A Parent's Guide to Multiple Intelligences* (Chicago: Moody, 2007).

Mothering Teenage Sons

Understanding the Process of Boys to Men

Neuroscientist and author Louann Brizendine uncovered some fascinating information while researching for her book *The Female Brain*. She discovered that the developing brain in both male and female fetuses is essentially the same until the eighth week. In the eighth week, there is a flood of testosterone that bathes the male brain, which in essence kills off cells in certain regions of communication and conversely promotes growth in cells in the area of sex and aggression.[1] Brizendine contends that these changes in the eighth week of life account for the obvious distinctions in men's and women's communication styles. And unbelievable as it seems, researchers have observed significant distinctions in communication styles in male and female infants

121

as early as just three months old. Their findings show that by twelve weeks of age, baby girls look to their mothers up to twenty times more than baby boys do to check for emotional cues.[2]

I wonder . . . is that why many women develop tight emotional bonds with their daughters well into adulthood? Is it from all that deep-rooted feminine response?

And I also wonder if it's that lack of the typically feminine response in the male child that leads mothers everywhere to worry and hurt over the way boys eventually pull away from them. Because about the time a boy turns eleven or twelve, he gets another big bath of testosterone, likely further enhancing the lack of interest in checking for Mommy's emotional cues. Most boys this age and beyond aren't particularly interested in checking in with Mom at all—either for communication or much else for that matter.

Mothers of young boys, here's a heads up . . . don't count on your teenager being a mama's boy.

The Previously Unnamed Hormone

I have to let you mothers of sons in on a little-known secret. There is another hormone that affects a boy's behavior. And though I am not a scientist and have never actually heard a pediatrician mention it, I have personally seen its effect in my own son. This previously unnamed hormone is the BO-MUC. Of course, that's an acrostic. The meaning? "Back Off—Man Under Construction."

The signs of this hormone's effect are unmistakable. They become bossy, bull headed, and exhibit various types of mood swings. They are senselessly sleepy and grumpy, even while getting up to twelve hours of sleep a night. (Or maybe I should say "a morning" since they are known to sleep as late as noon or one on weekends.) Quite often, these boys show a heightened sense of intellect. They are frequently all-knowing, possessing a wealth of knowledge and opinion about everything—as in, "No duh, Mom. I know I need a coat because it's cold outside. I'm not stupid"—but, at the same time, will display a startling sense of false reality. They have serious difficulty connecting simple things, like studying for a test and making a good grade. Seen signs in your son? It's really very normal—no worries.

This surge of BO-MUC is just another way to get Mom to back off and let the boy become a man. And though it is often the source of much hand wringing and heartache for mothers everywhere, it's a larger part of a glorious plan.

God's Mission for Little Boys

God's mission for little boys is for them to grow into men. They seem to intuitively sense that assignment when the hormones start to flow at the verge of adolescence. Their interest in becoming men is evidenced in all kinds of ways. They like to play rough-and-tumble games like football, soccer, and hockey. They typically disdain doing things that are considered distinctly feminine, whether that's cooking dinner or cuddling a baby. They'd rather dig a hole or fix a fence—anything at all that calls for heavy lifting, sweating, and grunting—than be caught dead planting a garden. They like taking risks, either in pleasure or pain, and will thrill at the chance for adventure. Frankly, little boys will readily imitate what they see men doing, whether healthy or unhealthy, just to be "one of the boys."

And because of that, many times they distance themselves from Mom. Psychological theories espoused by Freud and others would list numerous reasons for the maternal distance but for clarity here, I'll just mention one. Boys need to explore the essence of all things masculine. And they realize that the essence of masculinity is the polar opposite of femininity. So it just happens that while boys try and work out the equation of masculinity, they often see the need to distance themselves from anything that might wreck the process. And quite often, it's Mom. You know, the one that keeps double checking when her son is on the roof blowing off the leaves. Or Mom, the one that gasps dramatically when her son takes an elbow to the eye while playing basketball and jumps up in the stands, impulsively yelling out, "John! Are you OK?!?!"

Boys crave independence from the necessity of nurturing. What they see, as evidenced in the world they live in, is that

Femininity can never bestow masculinity. My mother would often call me "sweetheart," but my father called me "tiger." . . . A classic example of these dueling roles took place the other night. We were driving down the road and the boys were talking about the kind of car they want to get when it comes time for their first set of wheels. "I was thinking about a Humvee, or a motorcycle, maybe even a tank. What do you think, Dad?" "I'd go with the Humvee. We could mount a machine gun on top." "What about you, Mom— what kind of car do you want me to have?" You know what she said . . . "A safe one."[3]

John Eldredge *Wild at Heart*

real men don't need a mommy to take care of them. Which is actually pretty insightful for a kid of eleven or twelve. And to the extent that Mom doggedly holds on, reinforcing their littleness by bandaging every bruised knee (whether actual or metaphorical), they will be repulsed by her actions. Though on the inside they might crave the maternal attention, they understand that a real man is stronger than a mother's tenderness—or her disappointment.

The problem comes in when we as mothers get wounded in the process. And we often mistake a boy's need to pull away as rejection, when it's nothing of the sort. It's just a part of God's larger plan to grow a boy into a man.

A Boy about God's Plan

Even Mary, the mother of Jesus, experienced a feeling of confusion and disappointment with her son as an adolescent. Blessed as she was with a perfect preteen (Jesus literally never sinned), she still felt forlorn and emotional over Jesus when he was going about God's plans, from boy to man. There is a story that takes place when Mary and Joseph come to realize, of all things, that they had lost Jesus while traveling back home after visiting Jerusalem. And it's in this context that Mary experiences turmoil over her son.

> Every year Jesus' parents traveled to Jerusalem for the Feast of Passover. When he was twelve years old, they went up as they always did for the Feast. When it was over and they left for home, the child Jesus stayed behind in Jerusalem, but his parents didn't know it. Thinking he was somewhere in the company of pilgrims, they journeyed for a whole

day and then began looking for him among relatives and neighbors. When they didn't find him, they went back to Jerusalem looking for him.

The next day they found him in the Temple seated among the teachers, listening to them and asking questions. The teachers were all quite taken with him, impressed with the sharpness of his answers. But his parents were not impressed; they were upset and hurt.

His mother said, "Young man, why have you done this to us? Your father and I have been half out of our minds looking for you."

He said, "Why were you looking for me? Didn't you know that I had to be here, dealing with the things of my Father?" But they had no idea what he was talking about.

So he went back to Nazareth with them, and lived obediently with them. His mother held these things dearly, deep within herself. And Jesus matured, growing up in both body and spirit, blessed by both God and people.

Luke 2:41–52 Message

In this section of Scripture, more than any other, I find a lot of practical application regarding mothers and teenage sons. To me, it really highlights a process that is completely natural and right, though it sometimes catches mothers off guard.

I totally identify with Mary's mothering instincts. I mean, here's a kid who had his parents worried "half out of their minds." His independence and subsequent utter amazement at their reaction was so quintessentially teenage-ish. And then there's Mary's reaction, which was so quintessentially maternal. Don't you think you would say things just like that if your son went off and did something so heartbreakingly independent, worrying you to death? I know I would, and I actually think Mary exercised enormous restraint. I would have gone on much longer, wailing, crying, and shrieking. I would have laid on a total guilt trip.

But I think Mary's response to Jesus mirrors a viewpoint that should not be missed. Mary, just like the rest of us mothers, must have had a hard time making the adjustment of seeing her son as a man and not a child. And likely she struggled in remembering that Jesus would be about God's plan—not her plan—for his life. And I think that Jesus's response to Mary was a telling hallmark. The truth is that mother and son were on completely different planes here in Jerusalem. It's evidenced by the fact that when Jesus was questioned by his mother, he responded with, "Why were you looking for me? Didn't you know that I had to be here, dealing with the things of my Father?" Though I am not entirely sure what Jesus was thinking here, it's clearly evident that he was astounded by Mary's apparent oblivion.

She was bewildered by him. And he was astounded by her.

Can you relate? I remember many times when Will 3 and I would bewilder and astound each other through situations and conversations. And sometimes it would land us right in an argument. Looking back, I wish I had handled things differently, because I think it was my outlook that placed us in some of those conflicts. It probably had much to do with the fact that, regardless of his age or size, I still thought of him as a boy. Author Toni Morrison wrote in *Beloved*, "Grown don't mean nothing to a mother. A child is a child. They get bigger, older, but grown? What's that suppose to mean? In my heart it don't mean a thing."[4] How true. For in a mother's heart, her son—no matter if he's sixteen, 6'2", and 190 pounds—will always be her boy. And it's kind of tricky to change that line of thinking. It's hard to loosen that nurturing spirit, that emotional connectedness, and that maternal response, and let it shift to a new place. It's difficult to step back and find a new way to relate. Because in some ways you surrender a piece of your mothering soul when you release a boy to become a young man—and that can be painful. But it's paramount to his wholeness. And even though the transition is often tenuous, it is incredibly critical.

It's critical because it impacts how he views himself. It's critical because it sets the stage for future relationships in his life. It's critical because the ability to have a healthy relationship between mother and son hinges on it.

Acknowledging the process helps immensely. If a mom can confess that, yes, something is changing with my son . . . If she can acknowledge that he's different now, and so are we . . . If she can realize that because of that change, she needs to rethink the way she acts and reacts . . . then she will honor the wonder of what God is doing.

Facing In or Facing Out

But there is something else in the passage from Luke that caught my attention and is worth examining. Did you notice that despite the fact that both Mary and Joseph were frantically searching and that both were half out of their minds, when they finally found Jesus, it was only Mary that addressed him about their distress? Hmmm. Think about that for a minute as you imagine the whole scene. Here's twelve-year-old Jesus sitting in the Temple with these older men—the teachers of the Law or the Old Testament. I imagine that they are discussing ministry minutia and all kinds of glorious details about words and rules and so forth—the kinds of things that might make me very sleepy, like how I felt sitting in my Old Testament class right after lunch at Baylor University.

> Studies show that mothers typically carry babies facing in, cuddling them to their chest while fathers tend to hold babies facing out, to see the world.[5]
>
> Barbara Meltz,
> "With Baby Talk,
> Father May Know Best"

And there was Jesus right in the middle of it all. The Bible says the teachers were "all quite taken with him, impressed with the sharpness of his answers." No doubt they recognized a prodigy. But then, enter the frantic parents, Mary and Joseph. Mary's eyes likely widened and filled with tears when she saw him, and without thinking, she blurted out Jesus's name to capture his attention. Upon seeing his parents, he moved toward them as Mary rushed forward with arms wide open and pulled him tightly into her embrace. And it's then, after she's sure he's safe and sound right there in front of her, that she begins the rebuke.

But Joseph . . . he was quiet. No recorded words. No recorded actions. Just silent.

Of course, there is no way of knowing when or if Joseph eventually did talk to his son about the incident. I imagine that he did. But the fact that they reacted so differently as parents is just another indicator of the differences between men and women. And in this case, mothering and fathering a teenage son.

While Mary's focus was inward, with her attention solely on Jesus and her feelings of distress over the relational issues, I believe Joseph was focusing outward and sizing up the entire situation. Likely, he was looking at Jesus in the center of the room, surrounded by the wisest, most religious men of the day, through a lens of logic, piecing things together like a puzzle. He saw this twelve-year-old boy interacting with adults, well on his way to becoming a man—and an incredibly wise one at that. But not Mary. She saw the whole scene through the lens of her maternal instincts. Likely, she felt pure relief over how she recovered her lost son and was ever ready to tighten her grip to protect him.

Loosening Your Inward Grip to Tighten the Relationship

There is this tendency for mothers to focus inward in parenting. They are typically the ones who check for emotional cues from their teenagers. If a kid shows signs of wear and tear, Mom usually jumps in with an emotional thermometer to check the temperature and make sure everything's alright. And I actually think that God has gifted women at being extremely intuitive where that is concerned. But sometimes, that inward focus can blindside our ability to have outward focus and vision for our sons. If the mothering instinct is so strong that there is an inability to release the boy when he is moving down the path to becoming a man, then the relationship will suffer.

Preteen and teenage boys need to be free to become men. And that usually involves increased privacy, increased independence in decision making, and increased respect from their mothers. An adolescent boy needs to know that his mother—who is likely the most important female in his life, whether he admits it or not—thinks he is worthy and respectable. He needs to know that she thinks he is strong and capable. He needs to know that she believes in him, and he needs to see that her belief is reflected in her actions. It can be quite a paradigm shift for a mother who is used to parenting a little boy. And it's hard to change.

It's really a lot like exercising faith. Hebrews 11:1 says, "Faith is the confidence that what we hope for will actually happen; it gives us assurance about things we cannot see." In this case, you are looking at this teenage boy—a kid who can't remember to do his chores, exhibits careless disregard for his school assignments, shows no hint of work ethic whatsoever, and is entirely inept at basic social graces. You look at him today and think, "Mercy, I've got a complete mess on my hands! If I don't get busy helping him figure this out, he'll never turn into a bona fide man. He needs to be able to work a job and make a living to have a family! I've got to do something!" Your wheels are turning because it's time for complete and total overhaul via mother management, right?

Wrong. What you must realize is this: a stronghold of inner mother management on a young man's life communicates to him that he isn't much of a man at all, that he can't handle life without Mommy. And that is actually quite emasculating and embarrassing.

So how about this instead? It's time for some eyes of faith, some outward focus, and some assurance that God is in the business of making your teenage mess into a fine young man. You need some God-confidence about what he can accomplish. Stretch yourself out to God and ask him to help you shift your focus—looking out at the big picture. Ask him to help you believe that it's not all up to you. Pray that God will enable you to understand your role as the most important woman in your son's life, a woman who is looking on with complete confidence about what God is busy designing.

That might sound nice and easy in a nutshell. Real spiritual and all. Maybe even kind of meditative and passive— like you'd be sitting around just "letting boys be boys" and playing the part of the little woman. But that is not what I am talking about at all. I don't mean that your job is to sit back and become a passive, silent person in your son's life. Quite the opposite. I am asking you to consider being a woman who believes in him so greatly that you use every ounce of emotional and spiritual energy you have to become who he needs during this critical period of his life. And I am asking you to tell him that he's well on his way to becoming a man after God's own heart: strong, faithful, wise, and brave.

God needs mothers of teenage boys to grow to a place of incredible maturity so they can pave the way for God to do exactly what he needs to do to make a boy into a man.

Core Requirements

So what are those necessary elements required of you and me as mothers? What is God asking us to do and say and be busy about if it's not the whole nurturing-managing thing? Well, along with faith to believe that God will accomplish his glorious mission transforming your son from a boy to a man and along with communicating that faith to your son, there is one final matter. We need to be willing to take second seat to another person in our son's life: his father.*

Now, you might be thinking that sounds pretty unfair. I understand. But just to help you think it over, I want to pose a question: Who else will pass on a sense of masculinity to your son?

Author John Eldredge warns, "Sometimes, when the mother clings, the boy will try to tear himself away, violently. This typically comes in the teenage years and often involves some ugly behavior, maybe some foul words on the part of the young man. She feels rejected and he feels guilty, but he knows he *must* get away."[6] When a boy enters adolescence and begins his journey to manhood, he feels the need to disentangle from his mother and engage more forcefully with his father.

I won't soon forget when I took second seat in Will 3's life. There was a time in about fifth grade when, instead of talking with me about his day at school, I noticed that he waited until his dad came home to talk it over. And instead of enjoying conversation in the car on the way to and from after-school activities, he was pretty much silent. At first I thought it was some kind of phase that would soon disappear, but what I got instead was more and more of the same. There were many sessions of closed doors late at night when father and son were talking things out with no girls allowed—including me. And there were many days that I felt increasingly uncomfortable when speaking out and giving my opinion. What was once

---

*If you are a single mother raising a son, strongly consider and pray about introducing a godly male mentor into your son's life. It is God's design for little boys to have male role models, and though you can accomplish much for your son as his mother, only a man can pass on a sense of masculinity essential to becoming a healthy young man.

> Whether a child is male or female, fathers are needed for their "otherness," to put a healthy wedge between mother and child, to be a haven from real or imagined maternal injustice or excessive hovering.[7]
>
> Psychologist Victoria Secunda

considered sage advice regarding safety or preplanning was suddenly quite girly and silly.

I'll never forget the time when the two of them were heading out the door one day to go rappelling and I gave my standard word of warning, "Just make sure and be careful—double check the ropes. OK?" They instantly stopped what they were doing, looked at each other, and shared a knowing glance of exasperation. It was as if they suddenly had this transcendent man-to-man relationship connection flying way over my head that was leaving my heart trampled on the floor.

Eldredge sums it up this way: "This is a very hard time in a mother's life, when the father replaces her as the sun of the boy's universe."[8] And he concludes by adding, "Few mothers do it willingly; very few do it well."[9]

Moms, let's do it willingly and do it well. Let's release these boys to become men by trusting their fathers to pass on this mystery known as masculinity. But even more than that, let's trust *our heavenly Father*, the Creator of girls and boys, women and men. Let's surrender our hearts and affections to him, believing that he knows best. For it's only then that we can relax and savor the glorious process of watching our boy grow into God's man.

PARENTING YOUR TEEN

- What signs of BO-MUC (Back Off—Man Under Construction) have you seen in your son's life lately? How are these signs impacting how you are parenting him?
- Reread Luke 2:41–45. Jesus astounds Mary with his actions, words, and thought patterns. How does your son astound you in the way he thinks, speaks, and acts?
- Is there a chance that your reactions to your son's independence are bewildering him—just like Mary bewildered Jesus as a preteen?
- Do you recognize the tendency to have an inward focus in your relationship with your son? Are you able to spot an outward focus in the attitudes and actions of your son's father?
- Why is the concept of taking second seat so hurtful? What fears surface when you consider taking second seat?
- What will it look like for you to "do it willingly and do it well" in regard to releasing your son to become a man?

Mothering Teenage Daughters

A Map to the Heart of the Matter

I always longed to visit Paris. So when the opportunity presented itself for me and Emily to travel there through an educational program at her school, I jumped at the chance. The ten-day trip would also include various stops in Spain, from Barcelona to Madrid. But my heart swooned in anticipation over Paris, the City of Lights—the City of Love. Emily and I boarded the plane to France, ready for the experience of a lifetime.

When we finally arrived, I have to confess I was mesmerized. I stood in stunned silence while viewing the magnificent art housed in the Louvre and Musée d'Orsay. I was blown away by the Arc de Triomphe, then instantaneously dazzled and titillated by the shopping on the Avenue des Champs-Élysées. I stood in utter amazement, dwarfed by the magnificence of the Eiffel Tower. But it was Notre Dame that surprised me most. Gazing at the sacred enormity of the façade was breathtaking. The city truly holds some of the world's most stunning treasures. And because of that, I was absolutely certain that Paris would have me in tears over her beauty the entire time we were there.

I couldn't have been more wrong.

While I was in tears much of the time we were in Paris, it had nothing whatsoever to do with the beauty of the city. Instead, I was saddened at the lack of inner spiritual vitality. Here I was in a city with a reputation for "joie de vivre"—the joy of life—but found there was an obvious lack of any of the real and lasting joy given by God. Paris, though packed full of grand cathedrals, seemed to lack the Love and Light associated with God himself.

Although Paris holds the title of the City of Lights and the City of Love, it is clearly not of the spiritual nature. When asked about the spiritual climate in Paris, our tour guide explained that 90 percent of the population identify themselves as Roman Catholics, though he confessed that most are nonpracticing Catholics. As he put it, "We go to church three times in life—baptism, wedding, and funeral." When I asked him how that dynamic impacted the spirituality of the people, he seemed confused and explained that the moral code in France rarely reflects Catholic values. He said that the French are a nonreligious people. A three-day tour of the city confirmed that what he said was true. And I even sensed a sort of careless disregard from the people about the outward beauty of Paris.

Wherever we went, we saw trash. Cigarette butts littered the curbs, loose, tattered paper tumbled down the narrow streets, and even dog excrement was abundant, left on the sidewalk by careless pet owners. There was even a big stinking pile of it on the sidewalk in front of Notre Dame.

But the most distressing moment for me was reflective of the lack of moral values. I will never forget the evening we stepped off the metro, ascended the stairs (with twelve students in tow), only to face multiple stores offering sex-related services and products, all with blinking neon lights, in one square city block. There was the Sexadrome, Sex World, and the Sex Mart. The kids and adults alike stood speechless, eyes wide, as we somberly read one sign after another.

Frankly, it was heartbreaking. When I remembered the pictures I had seen flipping through travel books and compared that with the reality of the experience, I felt sorry that proud Paris lacked the engaging qualities associated with spiritual vitality. It was then I realized that my preconceived notions about the beauty contained in Paris and the realities on the city streets were at odds. And though the façades of the buildings managed to maintain a reputation for Paris, the inner heart of the city was woefully dark and depressing.

As I contemplated and prayed over Paris and her people, I realized that the desire and drive for outward beauty or a glamorous reputation at the expense of inner spiritual vitality was all too familiar. The whole situation was reminiscent of what I see girls and women struggle with on a continual basis. Beauty trapped in darkness.

All That Glitters . . .

We live in a culture that esteems beautiful women. We raise them up high as a golden standard. We photograph them at their best and highlight them on the pages of magazines. And yet, the more we pour into valuing the outward façade of a woman, the more we minimize the inward spiritual reality. And just like Paris, as we rely on the external appearances at the expense of godliness, we become dark and gloomy—void of Love and Light.

> All that glitters is not gold;
> Often have you heard that told. Many a man his life hath sold but my outside to behold. Gilded tombs do worms enfold.
>
> Shakespeare

This tendency explodes in adolescence, when physical attractiveness is paramount to social success. It's the cute, sexy girls who get the boys. And the beauty queen is the one who wins the prize. While all the world will stand on its toes to see a gorgeous teenage girl, they are not inclined to do so for the math genius. It's the way of the world—and especially for young women between the ages of twelve and twenty.

As mothers, our job is to tenaciously redirect our daughters to the truth about who they are in God. And that is no small task in today's culture. While the world tells them to work the façade, we need to continually remind them that it's the inner character of the heart that is valuable. While the world tells them to sparkle with sexuality, we must communicate and model how to shine as a result of purity before God.

Teenage girls need a model to lead the way—and it's not the one on the front of *Glamour*! Quite to the contrary, the most effective model is you. Though you might think that you are the last person on earth your daughter would take a cue from, you are wrong. She is watching you, taking notes about how to feel about herself and others based on your actions and reactions. Though she might disdain your taste in jeans and publicly distance herself from you when she's with her friends, she's keeping a secret diary about what it means to be a woman based on your behavior.

She's looking for a map to the heart of the matter: how does a woman look, act, and feel—what does it mean to be feminine? Psychologist Victoria Secunda put it this way: "A daughter is a mother's gender partner, her closest ally in the family confederacy, an extension of her self. And mothers are their daughter's role model, their biological and emotional road map, the arbiter of all their relationships."[1]

The bottom line is this: she's watching you and she's viewing the map. For better or for worse, your life is unfolding, directing her in the ways a woman should feel about herself. And this happens whether you are being strategic about it or not. As her body changes and grows—and her heart along with it—she instinctively senses the need to know the way. And tucked deep in that teenage heart is the need to understand her place and her purpose as a woman.

It is a mother's job to carefully lead the way on the often emotional journey from girl to woman.

Mapless in the Maze

Recently Emily and I were coming home from an event outside of Houston. She had accompanied me to a speaking engagement in Lake Jackson, Texas, that started on Friday and ended late Saturday afternoon. In an effort to cut some time off our trip on the way home and avoid the Houston toll roads, we took the advice of several attendees and went home a different route—one with which we were unfamiliar. We hurriedly pulled out of the church parking lot with directions scribbled on a Post-it note and a cell phone number from a local in case we got lost. Our whole goal was to get home to Austin well before dark.

We started out fine, but within thirty minutes we had twisted and turned ourselves into unsettling and unsavory territory. But we kept pushing on, hoping that the directions would get us on the right track. Another forty minutes later, with the sun setting quickly in the distance, I called the cell number to verify our directions, but no one answered. We drove on another twenty minutes, still uncertain when the back road we were traveling would lead us to the major roadway. After an additional fifteen minutes, I tried the cell number again, but it went straight to voice mail. With darkness stealing in all around us, I finally stopped at a creepy looking little convenience mart on the forlorn country road. I locked Emily in the car, rushed in for directions, and jumped back in with the good news that we were just twenty miles from I-10. As we pulled out of the graveled parking lot, assured we were going the right direction, Emily sighed with heavy discomfort and said, "We are never traveling without a map again."

Mothers, we must never travel without a spiritual road map. Understanding what the Bible says about becoming a woman of character is the only way to keep from traveling along mapless as we lead our teenage daughters through adolescence to womanhood. Don't be like me—on the way back from Lake Jackson, with penciled scribbles on a Post-it note. It's much too scary to risk letting your daughter get detoured, traveling in the dark.

> Charm can be deceiving, and beauty fades away, but a woman who honors the Lord deserves to be praised.
>
> Proverbs 31:30 CEV

Detour in Darkness

For several years I worked with Virtuous Reality Ministries, a ministry designed to help teenage girls understand and maintain their God-given worth and value in a culture hell-bent on doing otherwise. One division of the ministry involved traveling nationwide and providing events for teen girls and their mothers. Our team would come into a location—bringing a band, a couple of keynote speakers, and a bevy of workshop teachers—with the whole goal to permeate the message of purity and virtue in the lives of the teen girls.

While it was extremely gratifying work, it saddened me to see so many Christian girls, some as young as twelve or thirteen years old, torn to pieces and confused about their identity in Christ. Even though many made a decision to follow Christ as a result of experiencing his overwhelming love, they soon were knocked senseless by the cultural messages around them.

When talking with girls, I noticed two main messages permeated by society. The first message was related to body image. The message: You're not beautiful. This lie led many girls to cultivate a deeply rooted, distorted body image. The desperate desire to fit culture's standard of beauty led the girls to not only hate themselves but to also exercise extreme measures to achieve "perfection" as defined by the world.

The second message was to seek love at any cost. Many girls, some as young as twelve, had already surrendered their purity to boys in an effort to feel unconditionally loved. In essence, the girls were seeking love and acceptance regardless of whether or not that relationship weakened their moral standards or wrecked their dignity.

In my experience at events nationwide (and from my own life as a teenage girl), those were the two key concerns that managed to stop girls dead in their tracks spiritually—hearts trampled on the floor. They either felt that they weren't pretty enough (weight, height, hair, complexion, breast size . . . need I go on?) or they worried over a relationship or lack thereof with a boy. And the two issues were restlessly and continually entangled, leading the girls to severe darkness in their ability to understand their value and worth as young women.

In my estimation, it is that combo attack that manages the gravest fatalities in the hearts of our daughters. And the only way to counter the cultural message is to be a mother who holds the map, teaching and leading them to knowing God as Creator and Lover. Emphasizing that he is the only one worthy to hold their fragile hearts in his hands.

Knowing God as Creator

So let's just start here in an effort to understand what it means to know God as Creator. And since you, as a mother, need to take the lead with your daughter, let me ask you a pointed question. Please answer this honestly: Do you love your body? Or even more revealing perhaps would be answer-

> The American Society for Aesthetic Plastic Surgery reported that between 2002 and 2003, the number of women and girls younger than 18 who got breast implants nearly tripled. Doctors also say they are seeing more parents giving their teens the gift of new breasts or other cosmetic surgery for milestones like birthdays or graduations.[2]
>
> "Florida Teen Dies After Complications during Breast Surgery," ABC News

ing this one: Have you ever loved your body? If you cannot answer yes to either of those questions, I would venture to guess that you struggle knowing God as your Creator. The ability to love yourself—and the physical embodiment God designed just for you—is directly connected to knowing and appreciating God as your Creator.

In the same way we come to salvation in recognizing and embracing Jesus Christ as Savior, we come to love and accept our bodies, our physical selves, in recognizing and embracing God as our Creator. I feel that the gravest personal assault on girls today is the enemy's tactic to disengage girls from understanding their created worth and value by God.

If the enemy can trap your daughter (or you for that matter) into hating the image reflected in the mirror, he can widen the chasm of ever understanding God as Creator and she will miss out on the peace that comes from self-acceptance. She will also miss out on the joy of celebrating her uniquely designed person.

Psalm 139:13–16 is a passage that should be a required mantra for women of all ages. It says,

Oh yes, you shaped me first inside, then out;
　　you formed me in my mother's womb.
I thank you, High God—you're breathtaking!
　　Body and soul, I am marvelously made!
　　I worship in adoration—what a creation!
You know me inside and out,
　　you know every bone in my body;
You know exactly how I was made, bit by bit,
　　how I was sculpted from nothing into something.
Like an open book, you watched me grow from
　　　　conception to birth;
　　all the stages of my life were spread out before
　　　　you,
The days of my life all prepared
　　before I'd even lived one day.

Message

For me, the key phrase in that beautiful section is this: *I worship in adoration—what a creation!* What the psalmist here was saying is "I am marvelous! Fabulous! You made me just the way I am, down to the detail, and I am so grateful. I am in awe of what an outstanding job you have done with me!"

The psalmist is expressing the same awe we feel when we gaze at the vastness of the Pacific Ocean as it hungrily laps up the shore. Or when we're speechless at the foot of the Rockies as they stand like silent giants. It's the awe we feel when we look at the intricacies on a butterfly wing. Or when we marvel at the knowledge that every snowflake that falls from the cold winter sky is completely unique. It's likely the awe you felt after nine long months of pregnancy and

> Each second we live is a new and unique moment of the universe, a moment that will never be again. And what do we teach our children? We teach them that two and two make four, and that Paris is the capital of France. When will we also teach them what they are? We should say to each of them: Do you know what you are? You are a marvel. You are unique. In all the years that have passed, there has never been another child like you. Your legs, your arms, your clever fingers, the way you move. You may become a Shakespeare, a Michelangelo, a Beethoven. You have the capacity for anything. Yes, you are a marvel.[3]
>
> Pablo Picasso

hours of intense labor, when you finally saw that tiny baby girl you know as your daughter. Truly a miracle.

What we as mothers must understand is that, whether or not we mean to, we are leading and modeling acceptance or rejection of this whole premise of awe for our daughters. When we reject ourselves and the way God designed us, we are rejecting God as Creator. When we grumble about the shape of our face or the way our legs look in jeans, we're in essence saying, "Look what a crappy job God did here!"

You might think I am overstating things a bit. You might be thinking that being dissatisfied with your design is not that big of a deal to God. But it is. As a matter of fact, in Isaiah 45:8–10, the issue is addressed directly. Here's what it says: "What sorrow awaits those who argue with their Creator. Does a clay pot argue with its maker? Does the clay dispute with the one who shapes it, saying, 'Stop, you're doing it wrong!' Does the pot exclaim, 'How clumsy can you be?' How terrible it would be if a newborn baby said to its father, 'Why was I born?' or if it said to its mother, 'Why did you make me this way?'"

Knowing God as Creator means accepting his wisdom in your design. When we argue with him about how we are made, sorrow awaits in the form of a discontented, ungrateful heart. But when we examine the road map of God's Word and accept his directions as right and true, it awakens joy and awe. When you read Psalm 139 and acknowledge with the psalmist that you are wonderfully made—regardless of how you feel about yourself—you are aligning yourself with God's way of thinking. You read the verses and see eye to eye with God, knowing that he did something fabulous when he made you. He crafted you with a miraculous body (no snickering here . . .), and he crafted you with a distinct and amazing personality.

When you start to accept those truths as real in your life—and communicate that in your words and actions—you are modeling for your daughter what it looks like to acknowledge and appreciate God as Creator. And instead of wandering around in darkness listening to the enemy, you are shining a light for your daughter to walk in the way of her Creator.

From Creator to Lover

It took me years to really know and appreciate God as my Creator. As a Christian teen, I had many struggles with body image. I was completely obsessed with weight. I experimented with excessive dieting and had a bout of bulimia before I finally came to accept and appreciate how God made me. In those teen years, one pound plus or minus set the tone for my day. If I weighed 105 or less, I liked myself, thank you. But even a pound more—and I was fat and ugly until the weight was dieted or exercised away. My friends were no different. We all knew the calorie content of desired food items much better than we knew any important dates for an upcoming history final. To this day, I can tell you how many calories are in a small order of McDonald's French fries but would be hard pressed to remember something of more significant value like, say, the date of the French Revolution. Sad but true.

> Who are you, a mere human being, to argue with God? Should the thing that was created say to the one who created it, "Why have you made me like this?"
>
> Romans 9:20

Women young and old are weight obsessed, moms included. And though we have come to accept it as par for the course, there is a hitch. According to research at Penn State University, mothers preoccupied with weight encourage their daughters to develop eating problems. As a matter of fact, statistics now support evidence that girls as young as nine years of age fear getting fat.[4] And if that's not enough, girls are not just getting the "thin is in" message—they are also assaulted with the pressure to look "hot."

If you frequent the mall, I don't need to tell you what marketers are impressing on the tween set. In 2003 alone, clothing manufacturers sold 1.6 million dollars' worth of thong underwear to girls between the ages of seven to twelve years old.[5] And the onslaught affecting teenagers is even more pronounced. The last time I went shopping with my daughters, we were hard pressed to find dresses that were modest and stylish. The junior department was full of options, all of which had my girls baring a significant amount of cleavage.

This isn't news to you, but what might be is the fact that the intense, continuous pressure to be thin, sexy, and desirable stands in direct violation of what God the Creator had in mind for women. As Creator, he did not assign you a body with which to fight against in a love/hate relationship—to mistreat it to attain some kind of bizarre worldly standard. Nor as Creator did he assign your body to be regarded as "sexy" according to the world's standard. He did not mean for women to only be satisfied if they're deemed desirable by men. Instead, our Creator God meant for women to feel esteemed because of their intrinsic value assigned by him. He meant for women to know him as Creator and trust him as their greatest Lover. Isaiah 54:5 says, "For your Creator will be your husband."

The amazing truth is that when a young girl truly knows God as Creator, it is then that she comes to trust him as her greatest Lover. She knows firsthand his loving acceptance and then places her heart first and foremost in his hands. But if

There is an epidemic of low self-esteem, because parents haven't had the time it takes to build it. That has left adolescent girls prey to body image issues, so that none ever sees herself as good enough no matter how slim.[6]

Ellen McGrath, "Teen Depression—Girls: How to Get Closer to Your Teenaged Daughter and Prevent Depression" the enemy can convince a girl that she is ugly and unlovable, he has the potential to lock her heart in spiritual amnesia for a lifetime. And she will wander around seeking acceptance in all the wrong places, either by trying in vain to meet the world's standards or by placing her body in the hands of a man—looking for love and acceptance at any cost.

Don't let your daughter wander to womanhood without knowing her Creator God. Instead, bequeath her a rightful spiritual inheritance in knowing the acceptance and affection from the greatest Creator and Lover of all time. Model what it means to be a spiritually healthy woman yourself. Read the road map and believe that his directions will set you and your daughter on the right path. Truly it's the only way to get to the heart of what matters.

■　■　■　■　■　■　■　■

PARENTING YOUR TEEN

- How well do you know God as your Creator and Lover? Do you know what God thinks of you according to his Word?
- When you read Psalm 139, are you awed over how God created you? Are you able to marvel at how God has made your daughter? If there is a difference between your answers, what might be behind that?
- In what ways might your daughter's self-image mirror your own? How might you mirror your mother's self-image? Do you see distinct generational similarities?
- How does the understanding of God as Creator and Lover impact you personally? How could you use that

experience to direct your daughter as she approaches womanhood?

- Author Graycie Harmon said, "My mom is a never-ending song in my heart of comfort, happiness, and being. I may sometimes forget the words, but I always remember the tune."[7] What kind of tune will your daughter remember hearing in your life?

A Teen in Trouble

Keeping It Together When Life's Falling Apart

Last December, a seventeen-year-old boy in the Austin area decided he was up for a little risky business while his parents were away on a trip. Desperate for some action, he answered an online ad on Craigslist and waited for a female escort, who showed up at his door. He got a little more than he bargained for when the following day the woman and two of her "associates" came back to the kid's house demanding payment for services. The teen denied payment, saying that nothing happened between the two of them, but he was so frightened when they left that he made a phone call . . . to the police. The sheriff's department investigated the incident and used the kid's information to set up a sting, resulting in multiple arrests from prostitution to drug possession

153

charges. The boy, shaken and fearful, was not arrested (the "escort" finally conceded that nothing happened between them) but did get his story splashed across the front page of the *Austin American Statesman*. As Detective John Foster explained after interviewing the minor, "He got in a little over his head, I guess."[1]

Can you imagine your teenager in a newspaper headline—part of a prostitution/drug possession sting operation? Not the kind of thing you want future employers to know about—his or yours, for that matter. I remember reading that article, thinking, "Poor kid, his parents must just be dying. The embarrassment. The humiliation."

But the more I thought about this seventeen-year-old boy getting "in over his head" and calling the police, the more I realized it was the best possible scenario for him at the time. Because the truth of the matter is that there could have been a situation far worse for that kid than calling in the police and thereby exposing his mistake to the public—and that would have been not getting caught at all.

The Danger of Damage Control

When it comes to our own misbehavior, we all tend to think in terms of damage control—and that means minimizing the consequences for our misdeeds. No one screws up, then crosses their fingers and hopes for the maximum penalty. It's against our human nature. The truth is, we'd much rather just speed along the highway of life without an unwelcome interruption from a police officer. And when we do get caught, we aim for the lightest form of discipline possible. Honestly, most of us can come up with all kinds of tactics to attempt to avoid any penalty at all.

Remember what you felt like the last time you were pulled over for speeding. If you're like me, you stirred your creative juices and quickly came up with a couple of viable excuses for the police officer while he was walking up to your car window. As he checked your driver's license and insurance, you put on your most convincing compliant, remorse-filled face, hoping it might persuade him to have mercy and just give you a warning. Or if you're like one of my friends, you might have even turned on the tears to get out of that ticket. (By the way, she does this with great success!)

Damage control always seems like such a good idea at the time—anything to avoid the ticket. But the truth is that if the police officer issues a warning instead of making us pay the hefty fine for the ticket or take the lengthy defensive driving course, we are more likely to think we can get away with speeding again. And we're also more inclined to believe that we didn't deserve the ticket in the first place

This whole idea of not coming clean is not just a part of our human nature; it's actually a part of our spiritual DNA too. Refusing to "own up" dates back

> A sin takes on a new and real terror when there seems a chance that it is going to be found out.
>
> Mark Twain

to the beginning of time and is recorded in Genesis. It's here where we find Adam and Eve in the Garden. The beautiful Garden created by God where anything and everything is at their fingertips. A utopian environment with limitless choice and only one restriction from their Creator God:

No touching or eating from the tree in the middle of the Garden. Period. The end.

But it was too much for Eve. The snake tempted, then she tasted. Eve shared, then Adam fell. And voilà, the ingenious, albeit evil, invention of what we now know as damage control. Genesis 3:7 explains, "Right away they saw what they had done, and they realized they were naked. Then they sewed fig leaves together to make something to cover themselves" (CEV). When Adam and Eve recognized they were naked, they had two choices: fess up to the injured party (God) and face the music or figure a way out of the consequences and save face.

They chose the latter and tried to design a way out of their troubles, thereby creating the very first recorded act of damage control. Desperate to "fix" the problem and disguise the shame associated with their actions, they got busy sewing.

> When Adam sinned, sin entered the entire human race. Adam's sin brought death, so death spread to everyone, for everyone sinned.
>
> Romans 5:12

This whole idea of covering up mistakes isn't news to us. We see people attempting to avoid the penalty of wrong decisions every day, and teenagers are no exception. Kids mess up. Kids try to hide. We shouldn't be overly alarmed by this. As parents, I think the whole issue begs for discussion. So let me ask you an honest question: are you alarmed by your teenager's sins? Because if you are, that in itself creates a big nasty can of worms.

If you have a family environment in which a teen's issues, sins, whatever, are a big shocking, horrific surprise, then you are creating a very unstable, unspiritual situation for your kid. Your delusion about your little darling, the disbelief that he or she could ever do anything wrong, is at best an incredibly unrealistic situation. At worst, that kind of thinking tends to lend itself to damage control where you may in turn "sweep things under the rug," and that is particularly dangerous to a teenager's well-being.

See, the deal with damage control is that it evades the real issue. Everybody messes up. *Everybody.* And it's the reason Jesus came—to take final and complete dominion over this issue of sin and our need for cover-ups. As a matter of fact, this very thing is addressed with piercing clarity in Romans 5:6–11, which says,

> When we were utterly helpless, Christ came at just the right time and died for us sinners. Now, most people would not be willing to die for an upright person, though someone might perhaps be willing to die for a person who is especially good. But God showed his great love for us by sending Christ to die for us while we were still sinners. And since we have been made right in God's sight by the blood of Christ, he will certainly save us from God's condemnation. For since our friendship with God was restored by the death of his Son while we were still his enemies, we will certainly be saved through the life of his Son. So now we can rejoice in our wonderful new relationship with God because our Lord Jesus Christ has made us friends of God.

Damage control is a lame attempt to play the part of God in an otherwise helpless situation. The healthiest parents I know are the ones who realize that sinning and messing up are a part of growing up. They are realistic about the fact.

They know that it's an impossiblity to raise a sinless child, and they adjust accordingly.

Now don't get me wrong, it's not that these parents have a blasé attitude about sin—just the opposite. They are ever aware of it and its grave consequences. They are people who realize sin cost Christ his life, so they are abundantly grateful for the grace and its covering on their lives and the lives of their teenagers. They realize that the worst that could happen is not to have a kid's story of disrepute splashed across the paper. The worst situation would be to have a kid outside of God's great love and grace. And it's this kind of perspective that keeps their heads on straight when the inevitable happens—the teenager screws up.

The Problem with Becoming a Master Mom Seamstress

Although it's considered handy to know how to mend a pulled hem or reattach a button, there is one thing you never want to be good at mending where your teenager is concerned: mistakes. You don't want to be the person in

Interested in what is most effective at keeping teenagers out of serious trouble? The National Longitudinal Study of Adolescent Health found that the presence of parents at four key times of the day—early morning, after school, dinnertime and bedtime—is the best in preventing harmful behavior, such as violence, suicide, substance abuse, early sexual behavior and teen pregnancy.[2]

Dr. James Dobson *Bringing Up Boys*

their life who is adept at covering shame with proverbial fig leaves.

Recently I was flipping through a periodical and read about a mother who is an excellent "seamstress." I'll call her "Betty Sew and Sew." Mrs. Sew and Sew is suing her son's high school for five million dollars in damages because she believes they could have prevented her son "Junior" from fatally stabbing his classmate. She contends that if the school was doing its job, her son wouldn't be serving a penalty of twenty years in prison for manslaughter. School board president "John Astounded" finds it "bizarre that somebody expects the city to prevent their son from murdering someone between classes."[3] Sounds kinda bizarre to me too. While teenagers may be skillful at sewing fig leaves for themselves, don't be the mother who will gladly stitch up a leafy garment for your child. And although it's easy to see the irrationality of Mrs. Sew and Sew's logic, we just might be guilty of rescuing a kid from some other types of discomfort.

Has anybody out there finished *someone else's* English paper for them because turning in an incomplete paper would affect their grade-point average? Or how about feverishly completing an online defensive driving course because *someone else* didn't make time to get it finished? Or what about knowing that *someone else* dented up the car because they were underage drinking but lying about it to save face? They're all fig leaves, sewn up by a master seamstress.

The first real issue with being involved in covering for your kid is that it promotes deception as a viable alternative. Not something you want to teach your teenager at all. But Dr. Victoria Talwar, an associate professor at McGill University and a leading expert on children's lying behavior, asserts that children actually learn dishonesty from us. "We don't explicitly tell them to tell a lie, but they see us do it. They see us tell a telemarketer, 'I'm just a guest here.' They see us boast and lie to smooth a social relationship."[4] Or maybe they even witness Mom trying to weasel out of a speeding ticket!

The biggest problem, of course, with teaching your teen to lie is that it's unbiblical. And in the case of lying to cover shame, it sends the unsavory message that without some serious image management, your teenager just isn't acceptable. Not exactly what we're shooting for here, is it?

But the most damaging issue about sewing up fig leaves is that it wrecks relationships. Matthew Henry's exposition of the Genesis 3:6 passage has some incredible insight about what happens when we try and cover sin.

> The excuses men make to cover and lessen their sins, are vain and frivolous; like the aprons of fig-leaves, they make the matter never the better: yet we are all apt to cover our transgressions as Adam. Before they sinned, they would have welcomed God's gracious visits with humble joy; but now he has become a terror to them. No marvel that they became a terror to themselves, and full of confusion. This shows the falsehood of the tempter, and the frauds of his temptations. Satan promised they should be safe, but they cannot so much as think themselves so! Adam and Eve were now miserable comforters to each other![5]

Notice that Henry points out that Adam and Eve became "miserable comforters" to each other and that they were "full of confusion." When we, as mothers, act as accomplices, we can be assured that our relationship with our teenager will suffer. Though a teen might seem to appreciate the "help" in the beginning, he will grow to despise the duplicity. And it will confuse him. He will sense the hypocrisy and resent your expectation for duplicity between the person he really is and the person his mother is attempting to present to the world. Talk about a relationship killer. That, dear friends, is not unconditional love—it's some kind of screwy vicarious living.

Even more devastating is that when we try to cover transgressions, as Henry points out, God becomes a terror. When we attempt to hide our sins or the sins of others from a holy God, we become legitimately fearful of him. As we sin and feel convicted of wrongdoing but go scrambling for cover, God is no longer friend but enemy. Not one to whom we throw ourselves upon but one whom we hide ourselves from. We mimic Adam and Eve in the Garden scene in Genesis 3:8, "Then the man and his wife heard the sound of the Lord God as he was walking in the garden in the cool of the day, and they hid from the Lord God among the trees of the garden" (NIV). We hide from God. We hide ourselves and we hide our teenagers. And it is the last thing we need.

Whether we are in times of crisis or minor discomfort, we need God. And so do our teenagers.

If your daughter is caught cheating at school, she needs God. She doesn't need a well-crafted excuse defending her actions and blaming "the teacher's incompetence." If your son comes home drunk, he needs God. He doesn't need an aspirin and a sympathetic pat on the back because he's "just being a typical teenager." If your daughter comes home pregnant, she needs God. She doesn't need a lecture about using birth control followed by a visit to an abortion clinic to fix "the problem." As awful as it seems, the greatest truth in every situation is placing the entirety of the situation before our God. And it's in honest, authentic mourning that God will show himself to be our friend.

Comfort is found not in covering the sin but in taking the sin to the only one who can actually do something positive with a horrible, hopeless-looking situation. He asks for confession and repentance. And as a mother, you can model the behavior that maps the way.

Coping with the Consequences

I think one of the most difficult parts of parenting is allowing the hurtful consequences in the life of someone we love. Whether it's watching your son use his hard-earned minimum wage cash to pay for a speeding ticket or holding your outraged daughter as she weeps over a boyfriend you both know she should never have dated in the first place. Sometimes I think mothers bear the sorrow of their offspring with more remorse and pain than the children themselves. But what we must do is realize that the consequences for certain actions are in themselves God's way of parenting his wayward kids—your teenager included.

The consequences of sin are God's form of discipline. And it isn't his intention that we feel unloved because of them. Hebrews 12:7–11 explains it this way:

> My dear child, don't shrug off God's discipline, but don't be crushed by it either. It's the child he loves that he disciplines; the child he embraces, he also corrects. God is educating you; that's why you must never drop out. He's treating you as dear

children. This trouble you're in isn't punishment; it's training, the normal experience of children. Only irresponsible parents leave children to fend for themselves. Would you prefer an irresponsible God? We respect our own parents for training and not spoiling us, so why not embrace God's training so we can truly live? While we were children, our parents did what seemed best to them. But God is doing what is best for us, training us to live God's holy best. At the time, discipline isn't much fun. It always feels like it's going against the grain. Later, of course, it pays off handsomely, for it's the well-trained who find themselves mature in their relationship with God.

Message

The biblical reality is that if your teenager is suffering because of sin, it's God's manner of loving through discipline. And God promises that when that discipline is allowed to run its course—void of fig leaves—the result will be a closer, more mature relationship with God himself. Quite often, the best thing you as a mom can do is stay out of the way when the inevitable pain comes for your teenager. And just realize that if you can hold on, better things are ahead for both of you.

Engaging the Experts

So let's say you are reading along in realization that you have practiced the fine art of fig-leafing. And now you know that the best thing you can do for your teen is to step back and allow God's discipline. You are determined to back off so that you don't create more of a problem. That's good and healthy, and you should be commended, but beware . . .

But don't, dear friend, resent God's discipline; don't sulk under his loving correction. It's the child he loves that God corrects; a father's delight is behind all this.

Proverbs 3:11–12 Message

because while you might be ready to allow for the outcome, your teen might not be, and that in itself can create all kinds of hell. Truth be told, teenagers are expert prosecutors. They can reason and influence better than many seasoned lawyers I know. And because of that, they are well able to tug at Mom's heartstrings when they're suffering for their sins. Kids do a pretty good job of guilting good old Mom and Dad about how bad things get—even if they've brought it upon themselves.

We've had our share of sticking to our guns and being accused of being the "strictest parents any of my friends ever heard of." We've had our hearts and guts twisted to pieces, wondering if indeed our plan to allow for (and many times create) consequences for wrong actions is somehow too hard for our kids. I can't tell you how many secret parental meetings my husband and I have held behind closed doors, second guessing ourselves to death. It stinks to speculate and wonder if maybe you're actually stressing your teenagers beyond what's healthy. But for the everyday parenting woes (*not* for the biggies), we have come up with a little saying that helps in a pinch—we just say, "Write it down."

This statement, spoken in gentle jest, seems to deflect any ongoing guilt or blame. If the kids complain about how strict we are or how awful it is that we don't rescue them from certain consequences, we simply reply with, "Write it down in your journal." We explain to them that *when* they go in for counseling years later because their parents were so mean, kooky, and unreasonable, they will save time and money in those counseling sessions. There will be no repressed memories to drag up, no foggy dates and times; instead, my kids will have a chronological list of all our parenting blunders. They will have dates, times, and actual pieces of conversations to document why they are so messed up.

While our little saying is lighthearted, we actually only use it when someone's being pitiful (not when they are truly confused and suffering). There have been other times when we sought out help from mentors, grandparents, and counselors alike.

If you are in over your head with your teenager, talk to someone who can help you sort out what to do, what to say, and how to act. Glean the experience you need from people who have the wisdom to help. Do not hesitate to get in to see a Christian therapist with your teenager and hash things out. Parenting teenagers is not for the faint of heart, but it is for mothers just like you—who are determined to parent just like God the Father.

■ ■ ■ ■ ■ ■ ■ ■

PARENTING YOUR TEEN

- While the negative possibilities for teen misbehavior are infinite, how does understanding God's grace help you feel braver when you think of what your teenager could get entangled in?

- Explain in your own words the spiritual implications of damage control or fig-leafing.
- Why is a family environment where things are swept under the rug the worst kind of place for a teenager? What is communicated when you are shocked beyond belief by your teenager's misdeeds?
- How does becoming a "master mom seamstress" start innocently enough? What happens when that behavior is allowed to manifest into an expected mode of operation for a mother and her teenager?
- What two relationships are damaged when you act as a master mom seamstress?
- Author Stormie Omartian wrote, "If we go running into enemy territory and get shot at, we're not exactly being attacked. If we open ourselves up to the consequences of not living God's way, we shouldn't be surprised if enemy arrows pierce our lives. We've gotten out from the safety of God's covering."[6] What is the difference between you and your teenager being attacked and being people that have "gotten out from the safety of God's covering"? How does that difference influence how you parent your teenager?

Section Three

A Passionate
MOM

~ showing an intensity of zeal ~

Passionate Living

Lighting a Fire for Loving God

I am a recovering germaphobe. When my kids were little, I was the freakazoid ever ready with antibacterial hand wipes and an assortment of pleasant-smelling hand sanitizers from Bath and Body. I lived in utter panic that those invisible aliens known as viruses and bacteria would attack my children like *Invasion of the Body Snatchers*. My pediatrician didn't help the issue when he forbade me from taking my newborns to the grocery store. "If you take this infant to the grocery store and he develops a fever, I will be forced to give him a spinal tap to check for meningitis." No need to tell me twice.

I not only kept my babies in the house, far from the microbe-infected grocery store, but I also guarded them from potential germ carriers. That is to say, from other people. This included my husband's college friends who drove 200 miles to see Will 3 when he was born. The day my husband told me they were coming in for a visit, all I could think was, "Who knows what horrible bacteria they're harboring?!" So just to be sure they didn't contaminate my precious little newborn, I invited them to stand outside on our back patio and view him through the sliding glass window. It was the dead of winter and Will's friends stood shivering on our back porch, welcoming our baby through a thick, protective glass barrier. I am not joking.

Now, fast-forward a few years, and it was starting to dawn on me that my germaphobic behavior was well, um, odd. By then our second child, Emily, was born. And I credit Emily with forcefully breaking every hypochondriac rule I had ever established.

By the time she was two, she had discovered every gross and vile germ known to man. This kid, from the time she could crawl, insisted on being a doggie, or as she told us as soon as she could speak, "I mommy doggie big one!" She crawled around on the floor, barking and yelping and carrying all sorts of undesirable things in her mouth—just like a dog. And while I expected her to be grossly sick from all the contaminants, she was actually extremely healthy, while my firstborn suffered ongoing colds resulting in chronic ear infections. Emily broke the mold and helped me realize that germs aren't necessarily going to be the death of us all, contrary to my pediatrician's warnings.

When I woke to that fact, I realized by then that I had unfairly indoctrinated my small son with a huge amount of germ paranoia. So ever the inventive mother, I decided to undo all four years of germ propaganda with a quick romp to the park. We were living in Fort Worth at the time while my husband finished his seminary degree. And we were renting an older house that was right next door to a public park and recreation center. Typically the park was filled with kids from the junior high a few blocks away, but on this particular day, it was empty. Perhaps because for three days straight it had rained without ceasing and the playground was nearly submerged. Huge puddles of dark, muddy water lay under the enormous jungle gym like crocodile pits. And it was in those pits that I felt I could undo the mess I had made.

I excitedly proposed the plan to my husband: I wanted to take Will 3 to the park to play in the sandy, muddy mess and show him that getting dirty and germy is fun! I felt that if my son could see me dirty and smiling, somehow it would undo all those years of required hand sanitizing. My husband thought the plan was a tad bizarre and was unsure of the eventual impact, but he agreed to go along. He actually took a camera and filmed the entire outing. (Snarky man.)

I will never forget (especially since it is documented on video) running to the park and jumping and splashing around in the mucky mess, covered in wet sand from my head to my toes—beckoning my confused, reluctant four-year-old to join me. No doubt it was a puzzling moment (clearly one of many) for my firstborn as he watched his frenzied mother try to create a passion for mud, wet sand, and all matter of park-ish nastiness. His little face crushed in confusion at the drastic turn exhibited by his frantic mother as I danced in the dirt, enticing him to ignore the years of avoiding all things germy.

The fact is, I was faking my passion for those dirty germs—as evidenced by the fact that after about twenty minutes of "fun," I headed straight for a hot cleansing shower with my precious antibacterial soap. Though I had the right idea of trying to lead my son toward wholeness, the mark of hypocrisy was written all over my dirty face.

Faking Spiritual Passion

My abrupt desire to change course midstream with Will 3 is a lot like what I see frantic parents attempting with their preteens and teens spiritually. For many parents, the elementary years represent the calm before the storm. But when their once-compliant child enters adolescence and the raging hormones are stirred to a frenzy, parents sense an urgency in getting their kids to church.

Being completely entrenched in ministry for over two decades, it's a curious thing for me to see the resurgence of spiritual attention on the part of parents when their kids near adolescence. It's as if there is an internal alarm sounding off inside the heart of a parent, prompting them to action. Every fall, we see ambitious parents dragging reluctant, bleary-eyed teenagers to Sunday services. It's completely understandable that parents want the church to be a part of their teenager's life. There's the moral incubator element. You know, if they're good churchgoing kids, maybe they won't end up behaviorally experimental—making poor, impulsive decisions. And then there's the whole eternal insurance policy, just in case.

But if the parents are faking a passion for the church and the things of God, the moral incubation/insurance policy thing rarely works. Because while the church can provide programs and people to entice a young person to consider all things spiritual, if Mom and Dad are only coming to cheer the kid on but not participate, that kid will not be motivated. They're thinking, "What's the point? It doesn't make any difference in your life, so why should I believe it will in mine?"

Teenagers are experts at sniffing out hypocrisy. And they can cut through the bull faster than you can come up with some convincing argument to why it matters. The truth is, if you want a teen who is morally motivated and eternally secure, you are going to have to jump in the game and get passionate about God yourself. If you want a teen to value God, your chances of doing so are much better if you attempt to persuade her with your very life.

Now, if you are at the early stages of knowing and loving God, let me just encourage you here. Being passionate does not equal being perfect. Far from it. But it does mean that God is *the* important person in your life. It means that God is so important that you want to love and serve him with your life— and you desperately desire intimacy with him. And though that manifested desire might look a little different for every person, it is undeniably apparent when you see it. In the same way a person will throw all their energy and time and attention into a sports team or a hobby or an athletic endeavor, the God lover will throw that kind of commitment into all things spiritual. It's evidenced in the things they do and say in everyday ways. They are zestful learners, eager to please. And even when things get hard, they press in for more of him. Certainly, if there is a passionate lover in a family, everyone knows it.

Wholehearted Parenting

The Israelites of the Old Testament knew the importance of modeling a passionate love of God for their children.

> I lavish my love on those who love me and obey my commands, even for a thousand generations.
>
> Exodus 20:6

And they also understood that birthing a love of God and obedience deep in the heart of their offspring was an assignment straight from him. Instead of dropping an eleven-year-old at the front door of the tabernacle, hoping some good would rub off, they practiced the idea of a holistic faith that permeated all areas of life. They knew that once-a-week visit to the church wouldn't begin to educate with the intensity necessary to love and serve God adequately—and they understood that, because God gave them a detailed directive about how to accomplish this kind of wholehearted parenting.

In Deuteronomy 6:4–9, right after Moses recited the Ten Commandments to the nation of Israel, he reiterated devotion to God by pleading,

> Listen, O Israel! The LORD is our God, the LORD alone. And you must love the LORD your God with all your heart, all your soul, and all your strength. And you must commit yourselves wholeheartedly to these commands that I am giving you today. Repeat them again and again to your children. Talk about them when you are at home and when you are on the road, when you are going to bed and when you are getting up. Tie them to your hands and wear them on your forehead as reminders. Write them on the doorposts of your house and on your gates.

In essence, Moses was persuading parents to love God and then to transfer their faith to their children. And he was urging them to make the importance of faith an everyday occurrence.

The reality of an everyday faith is what teenagers need most. And though Sunday School teachers, ministers, and mentors can have unbelievable impact, parents have more—because it's really the unplanned moments in a teen's life that require the deepest spiritual illumination. Like right after school when the feeling of scholastic stress is fresh, or late nights when they finally verbalize that their sour mood was a result of how a friend crushed them emotionally. It's those unplanned moments that beg for a spiritual teacher. A person who acts as a spiritual linguist—able to explain and apply biblical truth in real-life situations. That's the job of a parent. And that's why Moses urged the Israelite parents to "write these commandments that I've given you today on your hearts. Get them inside of you and then get them inside your children. Talk about them wherever you are, sitting at home or walking in the street; talk about them from the time you get up in the morning to when you fall into bed at night" (Deut. 6:6–9 Message).

It's just possible that you feel overwhelmed at being able to "explain and apply biblical truth" or be a "spiritual linguist" for your child. Maybe it makes you quake in fear just thinking about it. Fear no further. You can become an effective spiritual guide by just staying one step ahead of your teenager.

One Step Ahead

I taught Theatre Arts at a classical Christian school for ten years. It all started when my high school friend and college roommate, Laura, secured a job teaching first grade at Regents School of Austin. My son was in her class. Laura was an incredibly innovative teacher who loved the students and the curriculum. And she was continually seeking new ways to engage her first grade class.

One day early in the fall, she suggested I come in and enrich the literature she was teaching with a drama component. Laura had seen me act in high school plays and knew that I was currently the drama director at our church, so she figured I would be able to add some drama to enliven her language arts class. The idea sounded incredibly appealing, but I had no idea how to teach first graders drama. I didn't have a degree in theatre or teaching. And any expertise apparent was the result of being a willing goofball with a passion to touch people through art. But the chance to teach in Will's class quickly beat out any apprehension over my inexperience. I went to a discount bookstore, bought some college textbooks on acting, and attempted to reformat what I read for a class of first graders. I honestly didn't know what I was doing when I finally took my "lesson" to the classroom, but the kids seemed to love it. And Laura thought it worked—so I quickly found myself volunteer teaching weekly in the first grade class at Regents.

By the end of the school year, I had made somewhat of an impression (the kids were my greatest fans), and I was invited to teach more classes—and they were going to pay me. I was flattered and horrified. Flattered because they thought I had done a terrific job and wanted me to stay and pay me, thereby making me a "real" teacher. Horrified because I literally knew nothing about what I was doing. If they could only see how I studied and googled and sweated over one little lesson for their first grade class, I thought surely they would reconsider hiring me.

But then I heard something that changed my thinking. I was in the office chatting with Nancy, a friend and founding member of the school. She was talking about the enormity of the task in creating the school (it was only one year old at the time) and finding teachers willing to reeducate themselves in the distinctives of the classical Christian mindset. I confessed to her that I felt pretty inadequate where teaching was concerned and told her that I really wasn't much of an expert. And I will never forget her wise advice. She said, "Don't be overwhelmed, Susie. The truth is that you don't have to know everything—you just need to stay one step ahead of your students." Can I tell you what relief I felt? All the pressure about knowing everything about drama and being an exemplary thespian swooshed out the door. All I had to do was stay a step ahead of six-year-olds. Now, that was doable.

> Train a child in the way he should go, and when he is old he will not turn from it.
>
> Proverbs 22:6 NIV

And friend, that's what you need to do too. Just stay a step ahead of your teenager. You don't need to go to seminary or be able to do an expositional study of the book of Leviticus. You don't have to call the pastor and get the okay on every bit of wisdom you seek to impart. But I'll tell you what you do need to do: you need to crack the Book and let God teach you about himself. You need to pray to love God with an unending, insatiable love. You need to love God passionately yourself.

Letting Love In and Getting Love Out

To be a passionate lover yourself, you must allow God to shower his love on your life. It happens when you diligently read his Word and pray. It happens when you acknowledge him as Creator every time you step outside and admire the great outdoors. It happens when you go to church and learn more about who he is and how he thinks. If you want to know someone, then spending time with them is the fastest way to do that. Spend time with God. Make your prayers conversational. Include him when you're "sitting at home or walking in the street" and "from the time you get up in the morning to when you fall into bed at night." Make God all of your life. That in essence is how to let God's love *in*.

Getting love *out* looks different. If you experience God's ongoing love *in* your life, it can't help but flow *out*. Unbelievable things happen in the lives of people that get on fire spiritually, because when there is a profound love for God, a love for others naturally follows. When the love of God flows into a person's life, filling it to the brim, it's only reasonable that the love of God will spill out.

This spilling out is evidenced in love for God and love for others. If you want to know if you're getting a God passion, look at your life. Is love evident? Do you see God manifested in your life and your family life? Is it a normal part of your family's existence? Remember, lighting the fire for your teenager is all about taking steps—even baby steps—in the right direction. And as you grow, letting God's love in, it just naturally happens that love flows out of your life as you share with people who desperately need it.

First John 3:16–19 illustrates this very idea. It says this:

We know what real love is because Jesus gave up his life for us. So we also ought to give up our lives for our brothers and sisters. If someone has enough money to live well and sees a brother or sister in need but shows no compassion—how can God's love be in that person? Dear children, let's not merely say that we love each other; let us show the truth by our actions. Our actions will show that we belong to the truth, so we will be confident when we stand before God.

The fruit of passionate living is passionate giving. And when you start modeling that in your family life, it has a boomerang effect.

How to Become a Fisherman

If you want really concrete advice about how to light a fire for your teen spiritually, staying a step ahead, then I would urge you to do this: become an expert fisherman. In Matthew 4:19, Jesus called out his disciples with this simple sentence: "Come, follow me . . . and I will make you fishers of men" (NIV). Then those men, just simple ordinary fishermen, dropped their nets to follow Christ. They followed him hither and yon all over the countryside, ministering with Jesus. Crazy? No, I think not. They were just passionate.

When you, the adult, become an expert fisherman, your kids will take notice. And they might just get so enthralled that they join you. It happens all the time.

Take Wendy, for example. Her parents are passionate

> This is the message you have heard from the beginning: We should love one another.
>
> 1 John 3:11

Christ lovers/followers, and she is too. Wendy is a senior in high school. She's a friendly, popular girl who likes shopping the mall and meeting friends at Starbucks for a chai tea latte. She goes to church and attends a Baptist high school. A neat Christian package. But last summer she felt a compulsion that, in honesty, was a little frightening for Mom and Dad. She felt that God wanted her to minister to people in Africa. So she did an in-depth Internet search, found a ministry group in Senegal, West Africa, got her parent's approval, then raised the money and went—alone.

Or Shane. His family has God's love spilling out all over the place. Captain of the high school football team, playing both offense and defense, he made a decision his junior year to miss the first game of the season because he had committed to a mission trip to Pass Christian, Louisiana. Instead of pleasing his coach (we're talking Texas, where high school football is a *big deal*), he headed out with his dad and some other men from his church to rebuild a dilapidated house for an illiterate elderly woman whose home was destroyed by Hurricane Katrina.

And then there's my eighteen-year-old, Emily. Raised a "PK" (apparently that alone can set a kid's teeth on edge), she has all the evidence she needs to know her parents aren't perfect. But she does know we're nearly nutty in our passion for God. Well, she's become a passionate God lover in her own right. Her heart breaking over the vagrants begging at intersections around Austin, she decided to take it upon herself to feed the homeless. After making a clandestine run to the grocery store for brown paper lunch sacks and food items, Emily filled them up and kept them in her car so she could hand them out to the folks begging at stoplights. (While I, on the other hand, feign toying with the radio to avoid eye contact with those very people.) Convicted by my heartlessness and her Jesus-like empathy, I offered to reimburse her for the grocery run, to which she replied, "No, Mom. I feel like I should do this myself."

What Wendy and Shane and Emily did was just follow a step behind imperfect, Christ-loving parents who tried to continually light the fire. And eventually those teens completed the cycle of letting God's love in and getting God's love out. See, they're really just regular teenagers whose personal passion for Jesus Christ is spilling out, making them great fishermen. And they're making their own imprint, impacting the world with his light. Because parenting teens with a God-sized passion creates the best fishermen ever.

I think we'll have to run to catch up with them.

■ ■ ■ ■ ■ ■ ■ ■

PARENTING YOUR TEEN

- How would you honestly rate your spiritual passion for God?
- What steps can you take personally to turn up the heat to becoming a passionate God lover?
- When was the last time you acted as a linguist (spiritually speaking) in the life of your teenager? Think through the process of how you identified the need for spiritual guidance and identify if you were able to readily apply God's truth.

- How can you stay one step ahead of your teenager spiritually? What steps in growth should you look into taking to ensure you'll model passion for God?
- What practices are present in your life that allow for you to let God's love in? What about your teenager's life?
- What practices are present in your life that demonstrate getting God's love out? What about your teenager's life?

Prayers That Make a Difference

Becoming Fluent in God-ese

The LAPD has a new communication device. It's called the *Phraselator*. This handheld contraption is effective at helping overcome language barriers in Los Angeles, "where police have long struggled to find officers who can communicate in all 224 languages spoken in the immigrant-rich city."[1] And though it's not as fabulous as the fictionalized universal translator on Star Trek, the Phraselator has the ability to translate certain phrases in up to sixty languages. This capacity has proven to be essential for public safety, especially regarding crowd control, natural disasters, and medical emergencies. As Police Captain Dennis Kato says, the capacity to communicate and overcome language barriers "can be a lifesaver."[2]

I'd love to have a Phraselator. It would be wonderful to use when talking with my husband, who speaks fluent Testostoronese while I speak Estrogenese. And it certainly would be helpful in communication with my teenagers. What mother wouldn't love the chance to have, understandable dialogue with her teen? That would keep any adolescent from stating the standard, "Oh, when you said that, I didn't know it meant that you wanted me to do that." With the Family Phraselator, there'd be no miscommunications, and families everywhere would be saved from relational disasters.

Captain Kato is right—the ability to overcome language barriers can be a real lifesaver. In fact, effective communication can mean the difference between life and death. No doubt, the Los Angeles Police Department comes face-to-face with that reality every day. And the truth is that if you are a Christian, you actually have access to your own Phraselator. It's a spiritual Phraselator, and it has the capacity to intercede with a direct line to God when you are at your wit's end with your teenager.

Your spiritual Phraselator isn't a handheld device; it is the Holy Spirit. He understands the language we speak, and

By the way I see things, God loves you the same whether you're being elegant or not. It feels much better when you are, but even when you can't fake it, God still listens to your prayers.[3]

Anne Lamott, *Traveling Mercies*

he also understands the language of God. When we don't know how to pray for our teenagers, the Holy Spirit jumps in on our behalf before God, making sense of our longings. He mediates on our behalf. Romans 8:26–27 explains, "And the Holy Spirit helps us in our weakness. For example, we don't know what God wants us to pray for. But the Holy Spirit prays for us with groanings that cannot be expressed in words. And the Father who knows all hearts knows what the Spirit is saying, for the Spirit pleads for us believers in harmony with God's own will."

I truly love that, because in essence the Bible here is saying, "Don't worry about messing up your prayers. The Holy Spirit's got your back. Just pray your heart out to God, and the Holy Spirit will cry out on your behalf, making sure your prayers are in accordance with God's will." For me, that is a huge reassurance. It's almost as if God is providing an insurance policy concerning my attempts at prayer. Whenever I pray, the Holy Spirit launches into action, translating. It certainly is gracious of God to provide such a system.

But there is another way to make sure that your prayers are on target for your teen. There is a foolproof way to guarantee that when you pray, you are asking in accordance with God's best purpose for your teenager. And the way you do that is to become fluent in the language of God.

Becoming Fluent in the Language of God

Right now you might be thinking I sound a little kooky. As if maybe I am about to offer you the option of "ordering my special online course, available only for the next ten minutes at a bargain price of $19.95, that promises upon completion you will assuredly become fluent in the *mysterious language of God*—guaranteed!"

No, I won't be able to provide you with any of that. But what I do want to do is to help you understand that God's Word—the Bible—has the capacity to aid your understanding of how God thinks, what God wants, and how he desires you to ask him for things. When you read the Bible, you learn more and more about what God wants for your life and for your teenager's life. And that wisdom makes you fluent. Then as you become aware of the truth of God and all the promises God has made on your behalf, you become confident. And finally, after reading the Word and becoming confident of the promises therein, you get really brave and claim those promises in prayer to God—that's when you are truly fluent in "God-ese."

So here's how you must begin: read the Bible every day. I know this sounds daunting—like a total language-immersion program—but stick with me just a minute and let me try to explain. The Bible is *the* answer to your questions about praying effectively for your teenager. Because when you learn how to pray for what God has already promised in his Word, that's when you'll begin to see some miraculous action in your family life. And that's actually a promise that I can guarantee, because the truth is that "the word of God is alive and powerful" (Heb. 4:12).

Now, I know how hard it is to try to read the Bible every day. I struggled to establish the habit for years, but I finally made it stick when I got a Bible that I felt was easily understandable. I found the *One Year Bible New Living Translation*. This Bible is set up with dated, daily reading sections, and this really helps me keep on track. Each day

God is not a man, so he does not lie. He is not human, so he does not change his mind. Has he ever spoken and failed to act? Has he ever promised and not carried it through?

Numbers 23:19

has a portion of the Old Testament, the New Testament, Psalms, and Proverbs. The daily reading takes me about fifteen minutes.

Previous to my *One Year Bible NLT* routine, I was a devoted Bible roulette reader. You know, where you hold the Bible upright on its spine, pray for God to speak to you, and open your hands allowing the Bible to fall open on the "anointed passage" just for you. The only problem with that was, I was pretty much landing on random Old Testament verses that read like this: "And when the body has a boil on the skin, and it is healed, and in place of the boil there is a white swelling or a red dish-white, bright spot, then it shall be shown to the priest; and the priest shall look, and behold, *if* it appears to be lower than the skin, and the hair on it has turned white, then the priest shall pronounce him unclean; it is the infection of leprosy, it has broken out in a boil" (Lev. 13:18–19 NASB).

That confused me, especially when I was so hoping to hear from God about coping with my teenager's lackadaisical work ethic. But ever conscientious, I would finish reading a section like that by praying, "Dear God, that is honestly the grossest thing I have ever read, and *I beg you to keep us from breaking out in boils.* Amen." No doubt there were many days the Holy Spirit was interceding and groaning (or laughing?) on my behalf as I begged God to keep us from all getting leprosy. Soon after that, I started trying to cheat the roulette system—kind of forcing the "anointing" by landing in the New Testament and Psalms. I was desperate for some answers about how to parent my kids.

While I had good intentions, I wasn't getting the big picture about God. And therefore I wasn't able to "hear" from him about how to parent my teenagers. The deal is that reading the Bible is paramount to understanding God. It's only by reading the Word that you start to understand the depth of his love and care for you. It's only by reading the Word that you start to realize he has good plans for your life. And it's only by reading the Word that you find out what those plans look like enacted in your life. Without the Word, you are pretty much a sitting duck where language barriers are concerned. It's not that God won't hear you—he will. But your capacity to hear from him will be obstructed.

The most fluent Christians I know are the ones who make a personal priority to read the Bible every day for themselves.

Colorful Dialogue with God

After finding a readable Bible in a translation that you understand and setting up some kind of reading game plan, you need to know how to start asking God for what he has already promised in his Word. There are tons of different ways to do this, and mine is only one. And honestly, while I share my little formula for how I end up reading and asking—speaking God-ese—my prayer is that you devise a system that works well for you and that you become really fluent.

Mine is what I call the "Two-Pen Dialogue" method. It works something like this. Every morning I get out my *One Year Bible NLT*, a lined journal, and two pens of different colors. (I have coffee too, but that's not really the point here . . .) Then I say a little prayer and ask God to speak to me. Usually something along the lines of, "God, open my eyes so I can

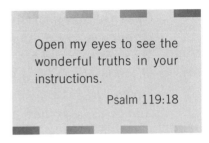

Open my eyes to see the wonderful truths in your instructions.

Psalm 119:18

hear you." Then I read the dated section, and as I read, if something sort of *pops out* at me, I write it down.

For example, recently I was reading along and this caught my eye in Proverbs 3:5–6: "Trust in the LORD with all your heart; do not depend on your own understanding. Seek his will in all you do, and he will show you which path to take." So right after I read it, I wrote it down in my journal with the purple ballpoint pen. (I always give God's Word a more unusual color.) After I finished reading, I wrote out my prayer in my journal in black ballpoint pen. And my written prayer was this:

God, help us to trust You. As a family, keep us from depending on our own understanding, but let us instead lean into You for the right path.

God, I ask specifically that You help Will 3 to trust You as he looks for roommates next year. Help him to really lean into You about where he should live and who he should live with. Give him godly roommates that will encourage his faith. I want to thank You in advance that You are going to show him what path to take by working all the details out.

And God, I ask on Emily's behalf that You would help her to trust You as she waits to hear about college acceptance. Please give her discernment as she waits. Open and close doors so that she will know which school is Your will for her. And come in close to her so she feels Your presence and peace. Thank You for taking care of all her needs, and thank You for the school that she will attend. Help us as parents to fully support her decision. And let us be excited about having two kids in college next year, not panicked about paying for it.

And finally, God, give Sara Your understanding of what she is supposed to do about the scheduling issue with doing both basketball and horseback riding. It's a lot, and she is confused about which is more important at this point. Please help her take this confusion to You. And I ask that as we try and help her sort things out— that You would really come through for her in a concrete way, helping her know how to handle the issue. Thank you that You will point her in the right path. And thank You for giving us the wisdom we need to parent according to what You want most for her.

God, thank You for the opportunities that we all have to trust You more. And thank You for promising to show us the right path.

Hopefully, what you see through this is a process of me reading what God has to say, then me agreeing and believing what God has to say. I am, in essence, leaning into the Truth, though it's yet to come to pass. I am believing that God will come through in all those situations because he promised he would. If you could peek in my journal, you would see pages and pages of purple and black, purple and black. God's Word and my words. A beautiful back-and-forth conversation as I

> Prayer invites us to rest in the fact that God is in control, and the world's problems are ultimately God's, not ours. If I spend enough time with God, I will inevitably begin to look at the world with a point of view that more resembles God's own. What is faith, after all, but believing in advance what will only make sense in reverse?[4]
>
> Philip Yancey, *Prayer: Does It Make Any Difference?*

"hear" him speak to me. And what is most impressive is that every year (often several times a year) I look back and see how God answered those prayers in my life. I'll be rereading an old journal and realize he answered a prayer, and I'll get a red pen and date or checkmark it to celebrate the answer. I have dozens of journals full of dialogue with God, and when I review them, I am astounded by his faithfulness to me and my family. No doubt about it—God comes through when I ask according to his Word.

My husband has another technique with equally amazing results. He reads the Bible chronologically, and when he sees a verse that pops out, he puts the name or initials of a person he is praying that verse for right there in the margin. If you flip through his Bible, you'll see tons of "Susie" or "W3" (for Will 3) or "ACF" (for our church, Austin Christian Fellowship), and all of this represents his directed Word-centered dialogue between God and himself.

Getting big prayers answered isn't as hard as you think when you ask using God's Word as a template. And while I still advocate jumping into the Bible all by yourself every day, I want to jump-start your God-ese fluency by giving you some verses that are great prayers for any mother, regardless of the situation. Below, in the "Parenting Your Teen" section, you will find the verses listed that I have used in praying for my teenagers—as well as myself.

My prayer for you along this journey is that you will find joy always, that you will *never stop praying* and that in all situations you will give thanks to God because of your relationship with Jesus Christ. And I pray that with assurance, knowing that it's the right prayer just for you.

> Always be joyful. Never stop praying. Be thankful in all circumstances, for this is God's will for you who belong to Christ Jesus.
>
> 1 Thessalonians 5:16–18

PARENTING YOUR TEEN

- Fools think their own way is right, but the wise listen to others. A fool is quick-tempered, but a wise person stays calm when insulted.

  Proverbs 12:15–16

- How can a young person stay pure? By obeying your word.

  Psalm 119:9

- It is foolish to belittle one's neighbor; a sensible person keeps quiet. A gossip goes around telling secrets, but those who are trustworthy can keep a confidence.

  Proverbs 11:12–13

- I will study your commandment and reflect on your ways. I will delight in your decrees and not forget your word.

  Psalm 119:15

- God has spoken plainly, and I have heard it many times.

  Psalm 62:11

- My child, listen to what I say, and treasure my commands. Tune your ears to wisdom, and concentrate on understanding. Cry out for insight, and ask for understanding. Search for them as you would for silver; seek them like hidden treasures. Then you will understand what it means to fear the Lord, and you will gain knowledge of God.

  Proverbs 2:1–5

- Guide my steps by your word.

  Psalm 119:133

- The teaching of your word gives light, so even the simple can understand.

  Psalm 119:130

- How blessed the man you train, God, the woman you instruct in your Word, providing a circle of quiet within the clamor of evil, while a jail is being built for the wicked. God will never walk away from his people, never desert his precious people. Rest assured that justice is on its way and every good heart put right.

  Psalm 94:12–15 Message

- My child, don't lose sight of common sense and discernment. Hang on to them, for they will refresh your soul.

They are like jewels on a necklace. They keep you safe on your way, and your feet will not stumble. You can go to bed without fear; you will lie down and sleep soundly.

Proverbs 3:21–24

- The godly people in the land are my true heroes! I take pleasure in them!

Psalm 16:3

- Get wisdom; develop good judgment. Don't forget my words or turn away from them. Don't turn your back on wisdom, for she will protect you. Love her, and she will guard you.

Proverbs 4:5–6

- When I was beleaguered and bitter, totally consumed by envy, I was totally ignorant, a dumb ox in your very presence. I'm still in your presence, but you've taken my hand. You wisely and tenderly lead me, and then you bless me. You're all I want in heaven! You're all I want on earth!

Psalm 73:21–25 Message

I remember my mother's prayers and they have always followed me. They have clung to me all my life.

Abraham Lincoln

14

The Final Exam

Learning to Let Go

I have had a lot of trouble writing this chapter. But there are many reasons for my procrastination. For one, I contracted some kind of mysterious stomach ailment. It was a little more exciting than most I've experienced. What started as a nuisance ended with a visit to the emergency room Easter weekend. And since my husband had already left to preach the Saturday night service, my twenty-one-year-old son drove me to the hospital and sat by my side as I answered the nurse's questions about things like my last menstrual cycle and my most recent bowel movements. Just the kinds of things no young man should have to hear about from any woman—especially his mom. Anyway, the mystery ailment kept me from writing for at least a week

195

as I went from one specialist to another, only to find out that there was no explicable reason why I was doubled over for hours on end Easter weekend. To add insult to injury, the mystery ailment was followed by a bout of viral bronchitis, which made sitting and typing nearly impossible. Between the exhaustion from the coughing and hallucinations from the codeine cough syrup, I stayed away from the computer for several days because who knows what I might have written. Oh, and lest I fail to mention, our air conditioner exploded yesterday evening, releasing gallons of water onto our new carpet. Sopping up all the water with bath towels took me away from my desk yet another day.

Yes, life was definitely making it difficult to write this chapter, but I was also beginning to wonder if maybe I was starting to suffer from a malady common to all authors: writer's block. Anne Lamott says, "There are few experiences as depressing as that anxious barren state known as writer's block, where you sit staring at your blank page like a cadaver, feeling your mind congeal, feeling your talent run down your leg and into your sock."[1] Honestly, putting off this chapter might have been a lethal combination of all of the above. Easily.

But then it happened. The real reason surfaced like a water moccasin gliding across Lake Austin—all dark and quiet and scary.

It appeared just an hour ago as I was fiddling around in my closet, trying to tidy things up. (Tidying is a devise I employ when a big deadline is looming.) As I was shuffling through books, clothes, and whatnot here and there, I noticed a book by Erma Bombeck that I had stuffed in a corner. I picked it up, casually flipped through the pages, and let my eyes quickly scan the words. And then, just like a snake, it struck me. Here's what I read:

> I see children as kites. You spend a lifetime trying to get them off the ground.
> You run with them until you're both breathless . . . they crash . . . you add a longer tail . . . they hit the rooftop . . . you pluck them out of the spout. You patch and comfort, adjust and teach. You watch them lifted by the wind and assure them that someday they'll fly.
> Finally they are airborne, but they need more string so you keep letting it out.
> With each twist of the ball of twine there is a sadness that goes with the joy, because the kite becomes more distant, and somehow you know it won't be long before that beautiful creature will snap the lifeline that bound you together and soar as it was meant to soar—free and alone.
> Only then do you know that you did your job.[2]

I put the book down and sobbed. I was shocked by the real reason I have put off writing this chapter. You see, the completion of this book is coinciding with the end of another job I've cherished—a far more important one—that of mothering my eighteen-year-old daughter, Emily. She is graduating from high school in a few weeks, and writing this book the last six months has served as a brilliant protection mechanism to keep me from focusing too intently on the reality that very soon "that beautiful creature will snap the lifeline" that has bound us together.

So I'm sitting here bawling my eyes out. Heaving and crying, trying not to let the tears and snot fall down on my keyboard. And all I can hear is my heart howling, "She's leaving. My precious little Emi is leaving . . . and things will never be the same."

Now, you might think I am being overly dramatic, that I need to give myself a kindly shoulder shake to force me out of my emotional state. But have you ever sent one off "to soar free and alone"? If not, it's possible that you've yet to understand how wildly things change when a teenager marches off into the world *to establish a life all her own*. Because it really never is the same. Never. Sniff, sniff.

Okay. I'm taking a deeeeep breath now and remembering that I have done this before and it's likely I will live. I watched our firstborn leave some three years ago, and not only is he thriving but I am actually thriving in his absence. It's not that I *still* don't break down now and then when I think of him, but I realize that my job with him is pretty much finished. And I also realized something else really important when Will 3 graduated from high school and went off to college.

The Final Exam

It was a muggy August afternoon in Waco, Texas, when Will and I drove Will 3 to Baylor University at the start of his freshman year. We unpacked all his belongings in the dorm room, made a Wal-Mart run for snacks and batteries, and finished our final meal together at a Chili's restaurant on campus. My husband, sensing my tenuous emotional state, forced a final goodbye between mother and son in the lobby of the restaurant. I think he thought maybe it would be easier for me if we were surrounded by people. But no such luck. I looked up at my son and immediately started crying. And then I hugged him tight, feeling that maybe

I *couldn't* let go of him, and cried even harder. With tears running down my face, I said, "Go . . . and have fun. I love you so much." When I finally pulled away, he looked down at me with his big chocolate eyes and said tenderly, "Mom, are you okay?" It was an unspeakably fragile moment for me. I wasn't okay, but I knew that he needed me to be okay. So I tried to pull myself together, put my hands on his cheeks, and begged (while still crying), "Go, *please go* . . . and have fun." I was clearly on the edge of mother hysteria.

My husband ushered Will 3 out of the restaurant, and upon their leaving, I really let it all out. Thankfully, I did manage to make it to the women's bathroom where I heaved and bawled like a baby for fifteen pitiful minutes. Afterward, I fished out my sunglasses from my purse to hide my blotchy face and went outside where I sat under a large oak tree. And it was there that I had a few brief moments of clarity about what was really taking place. Sitting there under that tree at Baylor University, I realized that I was taking a final exam—and I didn't want to fail the test.

This particular final exam comes for every mother. It comes in the form of a simple question atop a blank white page that reads

Will you let your teenager go?

The truth is that, whether we like it or not, we have to let our teenagers go. Literally. At some point, the course work is complete and it's time to let them walk out the door. A scary thought, isn't it? To be able to actually let them go and not resuscitate your old mom role takes a lot of courage. Tons of it. Because in many ways, it feels like a part of your heart is dying as they walk out the door, snapping that lifeline. And there is a strong sense of disconnect with everything you know to be true of mothering when you realize they are outside of your daily care. But what I have come to understand is this: As beautiful as Erma Bombeck's analogy is of kids and kites, we don't have to just release them into the wild blue yonder—free and alone—hoping they will successfully float away to happily ever after. Instead, our ultimate assignment is to commit them finally and completely to God's care. And we can do so with confidence, not with fear and trembling, because he is more than able to handle the assignment.

There is a wonderful little verse tucked in Acts 20 that helped me through my first exam in mothering. I call it the "goodbye verse" because of its context in Scripture. The apostle Paul had been ministering to the community of believers in the Greek city of Ephesus, but he felt "compelled by the Spirit" to leave for Jerusalem. After eighteen months of teaching, pastoring, and leading this group to love God, it was now time for a tearful goodbye. Paul gathered his spiritual family around him right there at the beach, with many weeping and grieving the fact that they "would never see his face again." And as he stood there with waves crashing in at his feet, he looked into their sad faces and said,

> And now I entrust you to God and the message of his grace that is able to build you up and give you an inheritance with all those he has set apart for himself.
>
> Acts 20:32

What a powerful goodbye. And what a blessing. Now, as I read that verse again, I realize it is just the thing I need to help me as I watch Emily go out into the world. She needs a powerful goodbye blessing, and I need the assurance that

God is going to take care of her. So that's the verse I am leaning into today and that has enabled me to write this difficult
chapter. I am not flinging her out into the big, cold world
just hoping all will turn out alright. Instead, I am letting her
fly into the arms of a loving heavenly Father who is able to
build her up in his Word. A God who has set aside an inheritance for Emily, an inheritance that is more secure than
anything I could hope to provide for her. And so I know that
whenever I feel compelled to over-mother my college-age
son or fret fearfully when imagining Emily away at college
in a few months, or if I seize up and get anxious or feel the
sadness overwhelm me, I will just remind myself that I have
already entrusted my teenagers to God.

And I'll know I have done my job.

Now to him who is able to do immeasurably more than all
we ask or imagine, according to his power that is at work
within us, to him be glory in the church and in Christ Jesus
throughout all generations, for ever and ever! Amen.

Ephesians 3:20–21

Notes

Chapter 1 Missing in Action

1. Anna Quindlen, *Loud and Clear* (New York: Ballantine, 2005), 7.
2. Virginia Rutter, "Whose Hell Is It? Why the Turbulent Teens Are So Tough on Families," *Psychology Today*, January–February 1995; http://www.psychologytoday.com/articles/index.php?term=pto-19950101-000023.html.

Chapter 2 A Proven Parenting Plan

1. "Barna Finds Four Mega-Themes in Recent Research," The Barna Group, 2007; http://www.barna.org/FlexPage.aspx?Page=BarnaUpdateNarrow&BarnaUpdateID=285.
2. George Barna, *Revolutionary Parenting: What the Research Shows Really Works* (Carol Stream, IL: BarnaBooks, 2007).
3. Anne Lamott, *Traveling Mercies: Some Thoughts on Faith* (New York: Anchor, 1999), 139.

Chapter 3 Stress-Free Parenting

1. Allstate Foundation at www.allstate.com.
2. Excerpted from SADD website, "Statistics," February 2007; http://www.sadd.org/stats.htm.
3. Foster Cline and Jim Fay, *Parenting with Love and Logic* (Colorado Springs: Piñon, 1990).
4. Valerie Strauss, "Putting Parents in Their Place: Outside Class: Too Much Involvement Can Hinder Students' Independence, Experts Say," *Washington Post*, March 21, 2006, A08; www.washingtonpost.com/wp-dyn/content/article/2006/03/20/AR2006032001167.html.

5. "Do 'Helicopter Moms' Do More Harm Than Good? 'Hovering Mothering' Has Become Common on College Campuses," ABC News, October 21, 2005, 1; www.abcnews.go.com/2020/Health/story?id=1237868.

6. Hara Estroff Marano, "A Nation of Wimps," *Psychology Today*, November–December 2004; http://www.psychologytoday.com/articles/pto-20041112-000010.html.

7. Ibid., 2.

8. Ibid., 7.

Chapter 4 Majoring in the Minors

1. Barbara Strauch, *The Primal Teen: What the New Discoveries about the Teenage Brain Tell Us about Our Kids* (New York: Anchor, 2003), xiii.

2. Ibid., 8.

3. Ibid., 6.

Chapter 5 Laying Down the Law

1. Hara Estroff Marano, "The Campus Crisis," *Psychology Today*, March–April 2004; http://www.psychologytoday.com/articles/pto-20040519-000002.html.

2. Marano, "A Nation of Wimps," 6.

Chapter 6 One Wise Mother

1. "Making Peace with Pop Culture," TheAntiDrug.com; http://www.theantidrug.com/E-Monitoring/pop-culture.asp.

Chapter 8 Overbooked

1. Jocelyn Noveck and Trevor Tompson, Associated Press Writers, "Academic Performance Top Cause of Teen Stress," MSNBC; http://www.msnbc.msn.com/id/20322801.

2. Peg Tyre, "Too Much Too Soon," *Newsweek*, September 11, 2006, 36.

3. "School, Study, SATs: No Wonder Teens Are Stressed" podcast, NPR Radio; http://www.npr.org/templates/player/mediaPlayer.html?action=1&t=1&islist=false&id=6221872&m=6221929.

4. Ibid, and Michelle Trudeau, "School, Study, SATs: No Wonder Teens Are Stressed," NPR, October 9, 2006; http://www.npr.org/templates/story/story.php?storyId=6221872.

5. Ibid.

6. Interview with child psychologist Michelle Kees, PhD, by Kara Gavin, "Is Your Child Overscheduled and Overstressed? U-M Expert Offers Tips on How to Tell—and What to Do," University of Michigan Health System website, July 25, 2005; http://www.med.umich.edu/opm/newspage/2005/hmchildstress.htm.

7. *Washington Post* Staff Writer Sandra G. Boodman interviews psychologist Madeline Levine in an article entitled "Sick of Expectations," *WashingtonPost*, August 1, 2006; http://www.washingtonpost.com/wp-dyn/content/article/2006/07/31/AR2006073100643.html.

8. Robert Yoon, "Exhibit Takes Visitors from Schoolhouse to White House," CNN .com, April 2, 2007; http://www.cnn.com/2007/POLITICS/04/02/young.presidents .archive/index.html.

9. "Biographies and Profiles: John F. Kennedy, the 35th President of the United States," John F. Kennedy Presidential Library and Museum; http://www.jfk library.org/Historical+Resources/Biographies+and+Profiles/Biographies/John+F.+ Kennedy+The+35th+President+of+the+United+States+Page+2.htm.

10. Interview with Marilee Jones, as quoted in Mary Beth Markle, "Getting into College Taxes Teens, Parents," *USA Today*, October 8, 2006; http://www.usatoday .com/news/health/2006-10-08-stress-book_x.htm.

See Marilee Jones and Kenneth R. Ginsburg, *Less Stress, More Success: A New Approach to Guiding Your Teen through College Admissions and Beyond* (American Academy of Pediatrics, 2006).

11. Quindlen, *Loud and Clear*, 11.

Chapter 9 Mothering Teenage Sons

1. Writer for *New York Times*, David Brooks, "It's True: Boys Will Be Boys," as quoted in *The Week*, September 29, 2006, 12.

2. Ibid.

3. John Eldredge, *Wild at Heart: Discovering the Secret of a Man's Soul* (Nashville: Nelson, 2001), 64.

4. http://www.quotegarden.com/mothers.html.

5. Barbara F. Meltz of the *Boston Globe*, "With Baby Talk, Father May Know Best," in the *Austin American Statesman*, June 16, 2007, A9.

6. Eldredge, *Wild at Heart*, 68.

7. http://www.poemhunter.com/quotations/famous.asp?people=Victoria %20Secunda.

8. Eldredge, *Wild at Heart*, 68.

9. Ibid.

Chapter 10 Mothering Teenage Daughters

1. http://www.wow4u.com/daughters/index.html.

2. Tanya Rivero and Jonann Brady, "Florida Teen Dies After Complications during Breast Surgery," ABC News, March 25, 2008; http://www.abcnews.go.com/GMA/ PainManagement/story?id=4520099.

3. Pablo Picasso, http://www.gaia.com/quotes/pablo_picasso_1.

4. PT Staff, "Facts and Tips: From Anger to Sex," *Psychology Today*, March–April 2006; http://psychologytoday.com/articles/pto-20060323-000006.html.

5. From Poll Watch, *The Week*, March 9, 2007, 24.

6. Ellen McGrath, "Teen Depression—Girls: How to Get Closer to Your Teenaged Daughter and Prevent Depression ," *Psychology Today*, June 2002; http://www .psychologytoday.com/articles/index.php?term=20030806–000003&page=1.

7. Graycie Harmon, http://ezinearticles.com/?14-Love-Quotes-To-Honor-Mom-on-Mothers-Day&id=539916.

Chapter 11 A Teen in Trouble

1. "6 Arrested in Williamson County Prostitution Sting," *Austin American States-man*, December 28, 2007; http://www.statesman.com/blogs/content/shared-gen/blogs/austin/blotter/entries/2007/12/28/6_arrested_in_williamson_count.html.

2. Dr. James Dobson, "Adolescent Rebellion"; https://www.family.org/parenting/A000001201.cfm. Online information excerpted by permission from *Bringing Up Boys* (Carol Stream, IL: Tyndale, 2001).

3. *The Week*, "Only in America Section," December 22, 2006, 6.

4. Po Bronson, "Why All Kids Are Liars," *The Week*, March 14, 2008, 45.

5. Genesis 3:6, *Matthew Henry's Concise Commentary on the Bible*.

6. Stormie Omartian, *Just Enough Light for the Step I'm On* (Eugene, OR: Harvest House), 65.

Chapter 13 Prayers That Make a Difference

1. Richard Winton, "LAPD Finds a Way to Connect," *Los Angeles Times*, January 16, 2008; http://www.latimes.com/news/local/la-me-translate16jan16,0,6435263.story?coll=la-home-center.

2. "It Wasn't All Bad" section of *The Week*, February 15, 2008, 4.

3. Lamott, *Traveling Mercies*, 120.

4. Philip Yancey, *Prayer: Does It Make Any Difference?* (Grand Rapids: Zonder-van, 2006), 210.

Chapter 14 The Final Exam

1. Anne Lamott, *Bird by Bird: Some Instructions on Writing and Life* (New York: Anchor, 1995), 176.

2. Erma Bombeck, *Forever, Erma: Best-Loved Writing from America's Favorite Humorist* (Kansas City: Andrews McMeel, 1996), 45.

Susie Davis is the author of several books, a radio host, a popular retreat and conference speaker, and a newspaper columnist. She has a passion for helping people love God and develop healthy relationships. With her husband, Will, she cofounded Austin Christian Fellowship in Austin, Texas, where he serves as senior pastor and she frequently teaches. They have three children: Will 3 (21), Emily (18), and Sara (15).

Visit Susie's website at www.susiedavisministries.com.